Landmarks of world literature

D. H. Lawrence

SONS AND LOVERS

D.H. LAWRENCE
Sons and Lovers

MICHAEL BLACK

Fellow of Clare Hall, University of Cambridge

CAMBRIDGE
UNIVERSITY PRESS

Published by the Press Syndicate of the University of Cambridge
The Pitt Building, Trumpington Street, Cambridge CB2 1RP
40 West 20th Street, New York NY 10011-4211, USA
10 Stamford Road, Oakleigh, Victoria 3166, Australia

First published 1992

A catalogue record for this book is available from the British Library

Library of Congress cataloguing in publication data

Black, Michael H.
D. H. Lawrence: Sons and lovers / Michael Black.
    p.   cm. – (Landmarks of world literature)
Includes bibliographical references.
1. Lawrence, D. H. (David Herbert). 1885–1930. Sons and lovers.
I. Title. II. Series.
PR 6023.A93S72 1992
823'.912 – dc20   92–8982 CIP

ISBN 0 521 36074 9 hardback
ISBN 0 521 36924 X paperback

Transferred to digital printing 2003

WG

Contents

Chronology

	Lawrence's life and works	Historical and literary events
1843	Barber Walker & Co. buy main shaft of Brinsley Colliery	
1846	Arthur John Lawrence born	
1850		Dickens: *David Copperfield*
1851	Lydia Beardsall born	
1857		Baudelaire: *Les fleurs du mal*; Flaubert: *Madame Bovary*
1860		George Eliot: *The Mill on the Floss*
1865		W. B. Yeats born
1870		Elementary Education Act passed
1872		George Eliot: *Middlemarch*
1875	They marry, 27 December	
1876	First son George Arthur Lawrence born	
1878	Second son William Ernest Lawrence born	
1879	Frieda von Richthofen born	
1880		E. M. Forster born
		Flaubert dies
1881		Henry James: *Portrait of a Lady*; Ibsen: *Ghosts*
1882	First daughter Emily Una Lawrence born	
1883	Lawrences move to 8a Victoria Street, Eastwood	Richard Jefferies: *The Story of my Heart*; Wagner dies

1885	Third son David Herbert Richards Lawrence born	Ezra Pound born; Nietzsche completes *Also sprach Zarathustra*
1887	Second daughter Lettice Ada Lawrence born Jessie Chambers born Lawrences move to 57 The Breach	Jefferies: *Amaryllis at the Fair*
1888		T.S. Eliot born; Kipling: *Plain Tales from the Hills*
1891	Lawrences move to 3 Walker Street	Hardy: *Tess of the d'Urbervilles*
1892		Whitman dies; final edition of *Leaves of Grass*
1895	George joins the army	Hardy: *Jude the Obscure*; H.G. Wells: *The Time Machine*; Oscar Wilde imprisoned
1897	Ernest goes to London	Conrad: *The Nigger of the Narcissus*
1898	Lawrence goes to Nottingham High School, to July 1901 The Chambers family moves to Haggs Farm, Underwood	
1899	Frieda von Richthofen marries Ernest Weekley	Yeats: *The Wind among the Reeds*; Mallarmé: *Poésies*; South African War, to 1902
1900		Nietzsche dies; Freud: *The Interpretation of Dreams*; Conrad: *Lord Jim*
1901	September–December, Lawrence works at Haywood's October, death of Ernest Lawrence December, Lawrence has pneumonia	Queen Victoria dies
1902	Pupil-teacher, to July 1905	Debussy: *Pelléas et Mélisande*; Arnold Bennett: *Anna of the Five Towns*; Conrad: *Youth*; Kipling, *Just So Stories*
1903		Herbert Spencer dies; Conrad and Hueffer: *Romance*

	Lawrence's life and works	Historical and literary events
1904	Wins King's scholarship	James: *The Golden Bowl*
1905	Lawrences move to 97 Lynn Croft June, holiday on East coast June, matriculation August, uncertificated assistant teacher at Eastwood, to September 1906	Wells: *Kipps*; Forster: *Where Angels Fear to Tread*
1906	Easter, first break with Jessie August, holiday at Mablethorpe October, at University College, Nottingham, to June 1908	Ibsen, Cézanne die; Galsworthy: *The Man of Property*
1907	August, holiday at Robin Hood's Bay October–November, writes first published story, appearing December in 'Nottinghamshire Guardian'	Conrad: *The Secret Agent*; Picasso: *Les demoiselles d'Avignon*; Forster: *The Longest Journey*; Joyce: *Chamber Music*
1908	June–July, sits final examination for teacher's certificate October, teaching post at Croydon, to November 1911	Pound: *A lume spento*; Forster: *A Room with a View*; Bennett: *The Old Wives' Tale*
1909	August, holiday on Isle of Wight September, meets Ford Madox Hueffer	First Futurist manifesto; Pound: *Personae*; Wells: *Tono-Bungay*; Ann Veronica; Hueffer edits *English Review*
1910	Writes 'Matilda Wootton', abandoned by July February/March to July, writes 'The Saga of Siegmund' 1 August, break with Jessie August, holiday at Blackpool; Lydia Lawrence falls ill ? September, starts 'Paul Morel' December, engagement to Louie Burrows: Lydia dies	Tolstoy dies; First Post-Impressionist exhibition in London; Yeats: *The Green Helmet*; Forster: *Howards End*; Bennett: *Clayhanger*

1910–13		Whitehead and Russell: *Principia Mathematica*
1911	January, *The White Peacock* published	
	February, 'Paul Morel' at p. 100 still; restarted March; 353 pages written by July	
	October, meets Edward Garnett; Jessie reads 'Paul Morel'	
	November, starts to rewrite	
	November–December, pneumonia	
1912	January, convalescence in Bournemouth, revises 'Saga' as *The Trespasser*	First anthology of Georgian Poetry
	February, breaks with Louie, resigns post, returns to Eastwood, continues rewriting of 'Paul Morel'	
	March, meets Frieda, has written two-thirds of 'Paul Morel', shows to Jessie	
	April, last meeting with Jessie	
	May, to Germany with Frieda: *The Trespasser* published	
	May, to Waldbröl, in June to Icking; finishes 'Paul Morel', sends to Heinemann	
	July, Heinemann declines the book; Garnett offers to read for Duckworth, Lawrence sends it, Garnett returns with comments, Lawrence begins to revise	
	August, Lawrence and Frieda set off across the Alps	
	September, on Lake Garda, revising 'Paul Morel'	
	October, changes title to *Sons and Lovers*	
	November, sends to Garnett	
	December, hears that Garnett will shorten	
1913	January, sends 'Foreword' to Garnett	

	Lawrence's life and works	*Historical and literary events*
1913	February–March, galley proofs	
	March–April, page proofs	
	May, reads Jessie's novel	
	29 May, *Sons and Lovers* published by Duckworth	
	17 September, published in the USA	

Abbreviations

Sources cited in the text by abbreviation and page number are

I   Volume I of *The Letters of D. H. Lawrence*
ET   Jessie Chambers's *Personal Record*
SL   Cambridge Edition of *Sons and Lovers* (by page
       number alone from chapter 2)

Full publication details are given in the final section.

Chapter 1

Genesis

Sons and Lovers, published in 1913, was Lawrence's third novel. Although he and his publishers were disappointed with its sales, it confirmed his growing reputation, and by the time of his death in 1930 it had been reprinted both in England and in the United States, and was the most popular of his works; indeed reviewers of his later novels fell into the habit of deploring that they were not like *Sons and Lovers*. It is now one of the most widely read of all English novels. It is usually the first book by Lawrence that anyone reads; often the only one; and is usually remembered with pleasure.

His first novel, *The White Peacock*, published in 1911, but started as early as Spring 1906 and redrafted several times in the interval, has important affinities with *Sons and Lovers*. It is set in the same region, the Nottinghamshire–Derbyshire borderland of Lawrence's childhood ('the country of my heart' he called it in later life), though the emphasis is on the natural beauty of the country rather than the man-made landscape of the coal-mining areas. It deals with a group of young people, very like Lawrence's youthful circle, about to leave home and enter life, and looking for a mate. It is tragic in that it suggests that their effort is thwarted and their life-endeavour will go to waste. They are blocked by things in their own nature which they do not control or even understand: in particular the sexual impulse fails or is misdirected. The men seem baffled; the women are powerful or dangerous. The reader who already knows *Sons and Lovers* identifies another Lawrence-figure, an analogue of Paul Morel, in the narrator Cyril Beardsall, who has Lawrence's mother's family name; one is not surprised to learn that Cyril's father is a drunken failure who left the family to be brought up by the mother. This diminished father-figure appears only briefly and is quickly killed off. Cyril is emotionally involved with, but unable to love effectively, a girl called Emily who lives on a farm; and we recognise the prototype of Miriam in the later novel, also based on Lawrence's boyhood friend and first love Jessie Chambers. Her brother George is admired, indeed loved, by Cyril; and his story is one of the leading threads of the plot: it is as if Miriam's brother Edgar (based on Jessie's brother Alan) has his imagined potential fictionally realised in this earlier treatment of the family − except that George too is tragically frustrated in his love for one woman and his marriage to another. An idealising glamour is cast over the whole novel, and one effect of this is to lift everything in the social scale, or at any rate to soften class characteristics. It is not possible to disguise the fact that George's family are small farmers, but Cyril's are positively genteel. Minor characters are allowed to speak broad dialect; it is as if the reader is taking a tourist's interest in local colour. The main characters speak literary English.

There still hung over Lawrence the anxiety he had expressed to Jessie Chambers in their discussions of his writing: '... what will the others say? That I'm a fool. A collier's son a poet!' (ET 57). He could not at first trust an overwhelmingly middle-class contemporary readership to be uncondescendingly inter-ested in the lives of people from another class; so we seem to be among E. M. Forster's people rather than Lawrence's. And yet his mother and the Chambers family were great readers: Jessie gives us a glimpse of her father reading aloud to her mother the newspaper serialisation of Hardy's *Tess of the d'Urbervilles*, with the hearer painfully involved, and shocked by the boldness of the author. In the event, a few perceptive contemporary readers of *The White Peacock* saw through the veil; for them it was an attraction that the modern novel, with Lawrence as with H. G. Wells, seemed at last to be widening its view of society; there were reviewers and journalists who were waiting for something they could hail as a 'working-class novel'.

Some of them were friends and colleagues of Ford Madox Hueffer (later Ford Madox Ford), the brilliant editor for a crucial couple of years of the *English Review*, where Lawrence's poems and stories were first published. Hueffer himself read much of Lawrence's early writing in manuscript, and was conscious of helping a new kind of writer with his advice as well as his patronage. He and his companion Violet Hunt were looking for accounts of 'how the other half lived' as Hueffer put it. For all that, Lawrence's self-protective instinct was not misplaced. There was an element of condescension even in Hueffer and Hunt, based on the inevitable class-conditioning shown by the unsigned review of *Sons and Lovers* in the *Standard* of 30 May 1913, which noted 'such terms as "protoplasm", "despicable", and "the human form" in the conversation of those who had not the habit of their use. Simple people have complex emotions often enough, but they are plain spoken or they take to silence.'

Among the early works which Hueffer read, the most notable was the first version of the story 'Odour of Chrysanthemums', published in somewhat revised form in the *Review* in June 1911. Here readers found the first treatment of a situation which recurs several times in *Sons and Lovers*, as it does in the play *The Widowing of Mrs Holroyd*, written in 1910, but not published until 1914, after *Sons and Lovers*. In the story as in the play, a miner's wife, with small children, waits in her kitchen with the evening meal ready. It is noticeable that she is not contentedly a member of the mining community; she corrects her son's dialect speech and in general seems too refined for the setting. As the time passes and her husband does not return at the end of the day-shift, she wonders if he has stopped off at the pub, in which case he will return drunk to a spoilt meal and there will be a sordid quarrel. Or has something worse happened − an accident at the pit? That is obviously tragic, and the reader from another class might, from a distance, sympathise; but in the first case, would 'refined' readers find an equivalent interest and sympathy? The final version of the story, published in 1914 in the collection *The Prussian Officer*, was the result of further and drastic revision *after* Lawrence had written and published *Sons and Lovers*. In its reassessment of the meaning of the bitter struggle between man and wife, it became one of his own indirect comments on the same struggle in the novel. But that had made him not just the recorder of a particular region of provincial English working-class life, but, as later readers began to perceive, the painfully involved author of a major classic of world literature, a landmark in a territory where other landmarks are Sophocles's *Oedipus Rex*, Shakespeare's *Hamlet*, Ibsen's *Ghosts* and, by way of commentary, certain works of Freud. For that reason we now tend to take the regional setting and the social realism as mere background, but they have importance, providing a particular and real setting which is also a social–moral world.

One glimpses this in another early story written in 1911, and first called 'Two Marriages'; it too was collected in *The Prussian Officer*, also much revised, as 'Daughters of the Vicar'. In the crucial episode, Miss Louisa, who might well be taken as representative by a female middle-class readership, finds herself facing a daily reality of the miner's family life: the young collier back from the pit in his alienating mask of coal-dust and sweat finds that his mother, on whom he is dependent for this service and much more, is ill and cannot wash his back. So Louisa, wanting to help, finds herself doing this task, which might be expected to revolt a fastidious young lady. But as she removes the veil of dirt she comes to the reality of another human being, wonders at it, and in due course unhesitatingly recognises her mate across the barrier of class (well represented by her parents' shock and resistance).

Another preoccupation in the early fiction, and another link with *Sons and Lovers*, is found in the early short story, published since Lawrence's death, 'A Modern Lover'. The surviving manuscript was written in January 1910. Readers of yet another short story 'The Shades of Spring', first written in December 1911, and included in *The Prussian Officer* collection, will recognise that in both stories Lawrence has returned to the beloved farm, the Haggs, where the Chamberses lived, and is as it were circling round the Paul Morel–Miriam Leivers relationship, or the Lawrence–Jessie Chambers relationship, and trying to imagine different outcomes. One has the sense of an account still painfully unsettled.

There is also a little group of stories — sketches really — which were revised for magazine publication in 1913, almost certainly planned as companions to each other, and probably thought of as exploiting the public interest aroused by *Sons and Lovers*. They had been drafted while he was writing the novel: 'A Sick Collier' in March and 'The Christening' in June 1912. They too treat of the daily reality of the life of the mining community. 'A Sick Collier' and 'The Christening' were included in *The Prussian Officer*; 'The Miner at Home', 'Her Turn' and 'Strike-Pay', also written in 1912 and revised in 1913, were published in periodicals at the time, and collected posthumously.

So too was the play *A Collier's Friday Night*, written in 1909 and shown to Jessie. In many ways it is the closest of all these early works to *Sons and Lovers*. It is obviously set in the Lawrence home: the father is there, washing, getting ready to go out on pay-night; the mother is there, the young student must be Lawrence, the girl visitor must be Jessie. The dialect speech is broad and vivid; so is the contrast with those who speak 'properly', and the setting is completely authentic. The play corresponds closely with pages 234—54 of the novel.

This family of fictions, or those which were published at the time, might have been received by readers in 1911—13 as establishing Lawrence as a working-class, regional, realist writer. There could have been some condescension in this public perception; there had to be a deeper interest; to find that, one had only to read a second time, and to start to make other connections between the works. There was in any case the second novel, *The Trespasser*, which breaks the pattern at once. Published in 1912, it was a work which imposed itself on Lawrence. It told the story of his friend Helen Corke, and her disastrous relationship with a married man, ending with his suicide on 7 August 1909. The body of the book recounts their six days' idyll on the Isle of Wight, out of the world, but for that reason thrown up against the limitations and failures of their relationship, which cause the man to kill himself. It is not at all a vindication of passion but another emotional impasse, another tragedy, more explicit than *The White Peacock*. The man, Siegmund, is utterly blocked, caught between a conventional jealous wife and his lover, Helena, who cannot really give herself to him. If the first two novels are taken together, there emerges from them a distinct aura of misogyny. Lawrence's feeling is invested in the male protagonists; the women they love have power; by denying the men they destroy them. Jessie Chambers shrewdly commented on *The White Peacock* that 'it seems to me not without significance that in this first novel Lawrence should portray no fewer than three men whose lives come to complete frustration, while Cyril [the narrator and Lawrence-persona] is a purely negative figure' (ET 119).

The Trespasser confirms the pattern. It was first drafted in February–July 1910, was shown to Hueffer, and submitted to Heinemann, who had accepted *The White Peacock*. But the advice Lawrence was given was that the book was unpublishable in its then state, for various reasons including its 'eroticism'; so he laid it aside, and thought he might not bother with it further. In any case, he was now seriously engaged in the writing of the third novel, which was to become *Sons and Lovers*; it was almost fortuitous that in early 1912 he returned to *The Trespasser*, rapidly revised it and let it go forward to publication. He needed the money it would bring him. The circumstances leading to that decision are best dealt with in the account of the writing of *Sons and Lovers* which follows.

At this point, the reader who has felt some confusion at this complicated sequence of titles and dates and draft states has had a practical introduction to an important aspect of Lawrence's writing: what one must call his method, even his aesthetic. Throughout his writing life he was working simultaneously on several things, each of which would be carried through a drastic process of revision after revision. So he would find himself working on one draft of one piece, while there was another which he might be revising in proof, and several short stories he was having retyped, perhaps, only to revise them again when he saw the typescript; and there might be something like *The Trespasser* written some time ago which he would suddenly take up again and completely recast. There was also a store of drafts of pieces written earlier, which might be taken up again if, for instance, a literary agent told him that a magazine was looking for stories, or a publisher offered to give him a contract for a collected volume, in which case he would revise the stories, often drastically. Between the works being written or revised concurrently, there would be an affinity or a continuity of preoccupation, because they were written while his mind was full of some particular concern or just because it was that time of his life. The underlying strata and the overlying layers of revision reveal a developing intention being gradually realised.

It was not a matter of his having a stated theme, still less a programme. Each draft was the product of a spontaneity; one could put this paradoxically by saying that it was his spontaneity that was programmatic. On the other hand, the redrafting — very often a sequence of radical rewritings — evolved a work where the successive spontaneities produce an effect which can be compared to that of a careful planning, except in the most important respect: Lawrence did not at the outset foresee all aspects of the end-product.

He was a publisher's nightmare in his way of working: every time he was shown the latest form of a work of his, he would not check that it had been accurately transcribed: that is, he did not check the new state against the previous one, so he missed many errors of transcription in the typing or type-setting. On the other hand he would obsessively revise, since he now saw aspects which needed to be changed, or was more in possession of what he wanted to say. Hence Lawrence's difficulties, recounted below, with those critics and advisers like Garnett and Hueffer, who made a fetish of 'form', and from that point of view judged his work on the assumption that the draft presently before them was a planned and final intention. He reached his own form his own way.

This becomes an important textual issue: the later editor of his work has carefully to plot his perpetually revising progress through a succession of documents of transmission and publication. There may be more than one manuscript, or a manuscript which represents several phases of writing and revision; then more than one typescript, usually made by a typist willing to correct in the process; then carbon copies differently corrected for publishers in England and the USA, then the proofs. It is fortunate that so many of these documents survive. One has to recover at each stage the new aspects of developing intention, at the same time eliminating the errors of transmission which Lawrence failed to notice, including his own, and the interferences by other hands. This becomes a critical issue: the interferences which Lawrence had to submit to in the process of publication included sexual censorship, which no modern reader is willing to accept; they also included changes made in the interest of formal standards — whether standard punctuation and grammar or the sense of literary 'form' which older advisers adhered to. This issue becomes important as we trace the history of the composition and publication of *Sons and Lovers*, and affects our own reception of the text which was restored in the Cambridge edition published in 1992.

One can sum up the early writings by saying that the regional setting and the working-class social background gave Lawrence a peculiar authenticity: this was where he came from. But that phrase in its modern use implies something internal. The collier's son who was surprisingly a poet and novelist was not primarily concerned to convey local colour, nor even, more seriously, engaging with 'the means of production', unless that is taken to mean the whole world which he re-created. The two first novels are unmistakably tragic, and the tragedy is located in the sexual relationship. The question arises: is this a personal, a social or a universal plight? There is an implication that it is universal. That might be a subjective overstatement, a youthful despair. If we press the question further, we see that the personal may be representative, and that is a better word than 'social'. If one feels, as Lawrence undoubtedly did feel, that one is emotionally blocked, it is sensible to ask, how did he come to be in this impasse, who else is involved, could they be called responsible, and does the story have a wider significance? Is it representative?

Lawrence's first reference to his third novel occurs in a letter to the publisher's editor Sydney Pawling, of Heinemann's, on 18 October 1910. Saying that he is not for the time being willing to have *The Trespasser* published, because he is not satisfied with it, he offers Pawling instead:

... my third novel, Paul Morel, which is plotted out very interestingly (to me), and about one-eighth of which is written. Paul Morel will be a novel − not a florid prose poem [i.e. like *The White Peacock*], or a decorated idyll running to seed in realism [i.e. like *The Trespasser*]: but a restrained, somewhat impersonal novel. It interests me very much. I wish I were not so agitated just now, and could do more. (I, 184)

Heinemann was at that moment producing *The White Peacock*; Lawrence goes on to say that he hopes it will be published soon, because he wants his mother 'to see it while still she keeps the live consciousness. She is really horribly ill. I am going up to the Midlands again this weekend' (I, 184−5). The reference to his mother's terminal cancer explains both why Lawrence wanted to be writing the new book, and why he was too agitated to do more.

His mother's illness declared itself in August, about ten days after his next-to-final break with Jessie Chambers − the coincidence perhaps struck him. She died on 9 December 1910: the painful account in *Sons and Lovers* can be taken as accurate in essentials. During those weeks Lawrence was almost completely preoccupied with her; one may guess that thinking about her and talking with her confirmed an intention to tell her story:

Sometimes as she lay he knew she was thinking of the past. Her mouth gradually shut hard in a line. She was holding herself rigid, so that she might die without ever uttering the great cry that was tearing from her. He never forgot that hard, utterly lonely and stubborn clenching of her mouth, which persisted for weeks. Sometimes, when it was lighter, she talked about her husband. Now she hated him. She did not forgive him. She could not bear him to be in the room. And a few things, the things that had been most bitter to her, came up again so strongly, that they broke from her, and she told her son. (*SL*, 429)

As if prophetically, he had earlier that year, some time before July, written forty-eight pages of a work called 'Matilda Wootton'; the unpublished manuscript survives as a completed first chapter and the beginning of a second one; it tells the story of a girl who was ten in 1860, describing her family and first years. The account is not unlike the pages on the early life of Gertrude Coppard in *Sons and Lovers*, including a time as a teacher and a first attachment like Gertrude's affection for John Field.

It is also the case that some time before March of the same year 1910 Lawrence had crossed out of *The White Peacock* a conversation between the mother, Mrs Beardsall, and her daughter, in which the older woman looks back on her youth, recollects a similar romantic attachment, and makes a complex judgement on her life: 'You have to determine whether you'll marry a husband, or the father of your children. I married the father of my children; a husband might eternally reproach me for it' (ed. Andrew Robertson, Cambridge, 1983, p. 370).

One wonders what made Lawrence delete that conversation, and what made him abandon 'Matilda Wootton'. Writing on 24 July to his friend Louie Burrows, who was now taking Jessie Chambers's place in his affections, he said offhandedly: 'As to "Matilda" – when I looked at her I found her rather foolish: I'll write her again when I've a bit of time' (I, 172).

The narrative instinct ('I will tell you') was sparked off suddenly again in a letter of 3 December to the poet Rachel Annand Taylor, a mere acquaintance. He explains why he is at home, and what is happening ('My sister and I do all the nursing'), and overflows: there is already more than a touch of art in the telling, and much understanding, born perhaps in the hours of watching:

I will tell you. My mother was a clever, ironical delicately moulded woman, of good, old burgher descent. She married below her. My father was dark, ruddy, with a fine laugh. He is a coal miner. He was one of the sanguine temperament, warm and hearty, but unstable: he lacked principle, as my mother would have said. He deceived her and lied to her. She despised him − he drank.

Their marriage life has been one carnal, bloody fight. I was born hating my father: as early as ever I can remember, I shivered with horror when he touched me. He was very bad before I was born.

This has been a kind of bond between me and my mother. We have loved each other, almost with a husband and wife love, as well as filial and maternal. We knew each other by instinct. She said to my aunt − about me:

'But it has been different with him. He has seemed to be part of me.' − and that is the real case. We have been like one, so sensitive to each other that we never needed words. It has been rather terrible, and has made me, in some respects, abnormal.

I think this particular fusion of soul (don't think me high-falutin) never comes twice in a life-time − it doesn't seem natural. When it comes it seems to distribute one's consciousness far abroad from oneself, and one 'understands'. I think no one has got 'Understanding' except through love. Now my mother is nearly dead, and I don't quite know how I am.

I have been to Leicester today, I have met a girl [Louie Burrows] who has always been warm for me − like a sunny happy day − and I've gone and asked her to marry me: in the train, quite unpremeditated ... When I hink of her I feel happy with a sort of warm radiation ...

Muriel [another name Lawrence gave to the Jessie-figure in some of the fictions and poems of his that Mrs Annand Taylor had been reading] is the girl I have broken with. She loves me to madness, and demands the soul of me. I have been cruel to her, and wronged her, but I did not know.

Nobody can have the soul of me. My mother has had it, and nobody can have it again. Nobody can come into my very self again, and breathe me like an atmosphere. (I, 189−91)

This is brave and honest, open in the way Lawrence was often able to be with people he hardly knew. With those close to him it was more difficult. There is a similar but less profound letter to Louie, written after a night of sitting with his dying mother ('Ada and I share the night'). It is 6 December, just before the end:

It is morning again, and she is still here ...

    I look at my mother and think 'Oh Heaven — is this what life brings us to?' You see mother has had a devilish married life, for nearly forty years — and this is the conclusion — no relief. What ever I wrote, it could not be so awful as to write a biography of my mother. But after this — which is enough — I am going to write romance — when I have finished Paul Morel, which belongs to this. (I, 195)

That thought, that what he was engaged on (he had written about 100 pages) was going to be 'awful', may explain the earlier false starts. He was now going to enter a painful territory, not just because it was a sad story about a blighted life, but because in really entering into it he would have to face what it had done for him and to him. He would also have to face the question: could he ever be free of that conditioning?

    On an impulse, he had become engaged to Louie three days earlier. One may speculate now that he felt that a new phase of his life was about to begin; that he needed to be married; that he felt an uncomplicated desire for Louie, who did not belong to his past in the way that Jessie did (i.e. was not, paradoxically, linked to his mother in their fight for him); and so the new phase should start with her. There is a dark underthought in the letter to Rachel Annand Taylor: he could never really love deeply again, and something like the desire for Louie would have to be enough. It is the first thought that emerges from the letter to Louie:

This anxiety divides me from you. My heart winces to the echo of my mothers pulse. There is only one drop of life to be squeezed from her ... And while she dies, we seem not to be able to live.

    So if I do not seem happy with the thought of you — you will understand. I must feel my mother's hand slip out of mine before I can really take yours.

He veers toward the underthought in a crucial statement:

She is my first, great love. She was a wonderful, rare woman — you do not know; as strong, and steadfast, and generous as the sun. She could be as swift as a white whip-lash, and as kind and gentle as warm rain, and as steadfast as the irreducible earth beneath us.

but continues hopefully:

But I think of you a great deal − of how happy we shall be ...
You will be the first woman to make the earth glad for me: mother, J.
− all the rest, have been gates to a very sad world ... We do not
all of us, not many, perhaps, set out from a sunny paradise of
childhood. We are born with our parents in the desert, and yearn
for a Canaan. You are like Canaan ... (I, 195)

In the last sentence the despair and the hope lie side by side.
It is possible that Louie responded to the remark about his
mother by saying to herself, yes, of course he loved her,
and so suppressed the true message. The day before his mother's
funeral, Lawrence met Jessie, and they went for a walk.
She records his insistence that he be understood by her:

... Lawrence looked at me with intensity. 'You know − I've always
loved mother,' he said in a strangled voice.
  'I know you have,' I replied.
  'I don't mean that,' he returned quickly. 'I've *loved* her, like
a lover. That's why I could never love you.' (ET 184)

1911 was a disastrous year for Lawrence. He started it grieving
for his mother. He had to return to his teaching job in Croydon,
work which exhausted him, and left him little time or energy
for writing. But he was now engaged to Louie, and she, being
the conventional child of watchful parents, would not become
his lover. They had to be married; and he had to save enough
to be married on; so there was a need to make money by
writing. The task before him was 'Paul Morel'; but the 'awful'
psychological cost of writing it was daunting. During the
year he revised a number of stories, and got one or two new
ones into first draft, but it was a painfully unproductive
time.

The letter to Pawling in October had said that the novel
was 'plotted out very interestingly' and about one-eighth
written. There is an outline in one of Lawrence's college
notebooks, and it is assumed that this is the original plan
of the novel. Here it is, slightly regularised:

I

I. Introduction – he pushes her out of the house before the birth of their son.

II. Tears without cause – watching the engines on Engine Lane – young sister Aunt Ada playing in Breach house

III. Sent to school – long lane young brother – Sunday school – super. Cullen Miss Wright – visit to Cullens – Newcombe lives there   Floss

IV. Move from Breach – Mrs Limb – Father hospital – Miss Wright making toffee in evening.

V. Return of Father – walks with Mabel – filling straws – visit to Aunt Ada

VI. Band of Hope – Fred strikes father – father blacks eye – Miss Wright – Fred in office – horse manuring – Mabel – painting

VII. Fred dancing – quarrels with father – Gertie teacher – Wm. learns from her – Flossie friends – Mabel jealous – Wm. at Mr Bates's school – painting – visit Aunt Ada

VIII. Death of Fred – Wm ill – Mabel – death of Walter Morel – Aunt Ada superintends

---

II

I. Wm. begins at Haywoods.

II. Goes to Miss Wright for painting – meets Flossie much & Newcome – reads & learns – neglects Mabel – she becomes engaged.

III. Advance at Haywoods – Miss Haywood & painting (red-haired Pauline) – Newcome very jealous

IV. Flossie passes high – renewed attention of Wm. – great friendship after painting in Castle – death of Miss Wright.

V. Flossie in College – death of Miss Wright

This is interesting from more than one point of view. Given what was said above about Lawrence's successive spontaneities, one would not expect him to work to a plan at all. In fact only one other similar document survives, a fragmentary note for part of 'Laetitia', an early version of *The White Peacock*. It is reasonable to infer that as he went on writing Lawrence discovered his method, and that he dropped, if he ever really formed, the habit of making a plan. The obvious critical or aesthetic disadvantage is that a too-much considered plan, followed too closely, prevents writers from discovering as they go along what it is they really want to say; with a plan rigidly adhered to, you only produce at the end what you projected at the beginning, and the work itself is not allowed to tell you where it needs to go. From the start, Lawrence had an instinctive sense of this issue; Jessie remembers him saying, when he was thinking about *The White Peacock*:

The usual plan is to take two couples and develop their relationships ... Most of George Eliot's are on that plan. Anyhow, I don't want a plot, I should be bored with it. (ET 103)

Many readers are familiar with his later statement that 'the novels and poems come unwatched out of one's pen', so that he felt he had to write his discursive or philosophical works in order to develop more consciously what the imaginative works were doing in the other way. Similarly, one may remember the passage in a letter of 23 April 1913, when he had embarked on his most prolonged and complicated piece of writing, the novel which finally split into *The Rainbow* and *Women in Love*: 'I am doing a novel which I have never grasped. Damn its eyes, there I am at page 145, and I've no notion what it's about. I hate it. F[rieda] says it is good. But it's like a novel in a foreign language I don't know very well — I can only just make out what it is about' (I, 544). There is a clear affinity here with things said about *Sons and Lovers* itself — compare for instance, Frieda's penetrating remarks about 'form' in the letter to Garnett quoted below.

In fact, there is a cardinal aspect of much twentieth-century art involved here. What Lawrence finally entered on as a way of working suited what he called his 'demon' — the creative element of his nature which knew better than his conscious mind or social intelligence what he had to say. There is an important statement written when he was forty-two, but looking back to his early life:

... I remember the slightly self-conscious Sunday afternoon, when I was nineteen [twenty, actually], and I 'composed' my first two

'poems' ... most young ladies would have done better: at least
I hope so. But I thought the effusions very nice, and so did Miriam.
   Then much more vaguely I remember subsequent half-furtive
moments when I would absorbedly scribble at verse for an hour
or so, and then run away from that act and the production as if
it were secret sin ... I used to feel myself at times haunted by something, and a little guilty about it, as if it were an abnormality. Then
the haunting would get the better of me, and the ghost would suddenly
appear, in the shape of a usually rather incoherent poem. Nearly
always I shunned the apparition once it had appeared. From the
first, I was a little afraid of my real poems — not my 'compositions,'
but the poems that had the ghost in them. They seemed to me to
come from somewhere, I didn't quite know where, out of a me
whom I didn't know and didn't want to know, and to say things
I would much rather not have said: for choice. But there they
were ...
   To this day, I still have the uneasy haunted feeling, and would
rather not write most of the things I do write ... Only now I know
my demon better, and, after bitter years, respect him more than
my other, milder and nicer self.

Then, a few lines later, a crucial remark about the process
of revision:

It is not for technique these poems are altered: it is to say the real
say ... The demon, when he's really there, makes his own form
willy-nilly, and is unchangeable. ('Foreword' to *Collected Poems*,
printed as Appendix I in *The Complete Poems*, ed. Vivian de Sola
Pinto and Warren Roberts, 1964, pp. 849–51)

   Lawrence's insight — his working method — was theorised
later in the century, first by the Surrealists, and then by the
Abstract Expressionists, as the liberation of the subconscious.
That formal psychoanalytical appropriation of the process
disguises an older Romantic approach: 'inspiration' is now
thought to be a discredited idea, 'romantic' in a weak sense.
But the old idea of a 'muse' who stood apart from the poet
and dictated to him what he was to say catches the same
idea of something coming from a source which because it
was deeper, seemed other.
   Blake had said of his pictures, 'Though I call them mine,
yet I know that they are not mine'. F.R. Leavis in his last
book on Lawrence, pondering the relationship with Blake,

also wanting to theorise the creative process, but seeking to escape the narrowly Freudian terms of Surrealism and after, felicitously expressed the whole composition process as 'the emergence, as he [Lawrence] experienced it, of original thought out of the ungrasped apprehended − the intuitively, the vaguely but insistently apprehended: first the stir of apprehension, and then the prolonged repetitious wrestle to persuade it into words' (*Thought, Words and Creativity*, 1976, p. 124). Leavis also saw that this process was not merely internal to, and completed in, each separate work; it was the basic impulsion of the whole life-work, in which each new start was a further attempt to catch an aspect of the whole. The extraordinary sequence of successive drafts of successive works may be reductively described as simply crystallising into the works of D. H. Lawrence, seen from outside as the row of volumes on the shelf. Received internally and related in the same way as they were conceived, they are 'a unity, a coherent organic and comprehensive totality' (p. 67).

In fact, to return to the interestingly 'plotted out' first sketch of 'Paul Morel', there is no conflict with the theory, or with the concept of Lawrence as an instinctive writer. Parts of the scheme were abandoned or overtaken by Lawrence's own reconceiving as he went along, so that the plan represents − could only represent − one stage in the evolution of the novel. It is as unlike the final version as the plan for 'Laetitia' was unlike *The White Peacock* in its final form. What we have in both cases is a set of very brief notes, not much more than a memorandum of incidents and characters. In particular there is very little that a nineteenth-century novelist would recognise as 'plot', i.e. those complex devices of incident, coincidence, change of fortune, hidden relationships, sudden discovery and so on which enabled a popular writer to introduce a large cast of characters, set them working on each other, and bring them to a happy or tragic ending, with everything satisfactorily 'worked out'. Nor is there any statement of 'theme'. What we have is consonant with Lawrence's very simple narrative procedure, which seems, like his prose, paratactic. His natural unit is the long chapter in which there are a number of scenes or incidents connected by the sense that these things are narrated in this order because 'that is how it was'. The implied syntax of the chapter is not hierarchical: the ordering (as in the Bible) is 'and then, ... and then, ... and then ...' That procedure allows for the maximum of what seems in *Sons and Lovers* to be unforced remembering – except of course that the process is much more complex than that: a profound reshaping is hidden in the simple telling, and the recurrences which do actually give a higher structure may seem no more than the natural recurrences which occur in every life. The other profound but mysterious structural principle, the tissue of imagery, is not even hinted at in the plan, because it is not so much Lawrence's way of writing as his way of thinking.

Some of the names in the plan are those of people Lawrence knew as a boy. He had been fond of the girl Mabel Limb who had died of cancer a year before his mother, and the name Limb occurs in the completed novel; the Cullens were well-known in Eastwood, and Flossie Cullen and Miss Wright were later to be the prototypes of Alvina Houghton and Miss Frost in *The Lost Girl* (1920). The interesting and important feature of the plan, a truly structural principle which persists throughout the writing of the novel, is that there are two parts; that an older brother, here called Fred, seems to be given prominence in Part I; that it ends with his death and the illness of the younger brother, here called William. In Part II William is the central figure, but Flossie becomes important and seems to be evolving into a prototype of Miriam in *Sons and Lovers*, possibly of Ursula in *The Rainbow*. The father, already called Walter Morel, dies at the end of Part I, before William takes the foreground – is therefore disposed of much as the father-figure is disposed of in *The White Peacock*. Most significantly, the plan says nothing about the mother-figure in Part II, and she occurs in Part I only as a mysterious 'her'; one wonders whether that is because it was too 'awful' at this point to contemplate a struggle between son, mother and lover. If the plan was jotted down before August 1910, Mrs Lawrence was not yet ill, and Lawrence did not yet have to contemplate her death, an obvious end to the story, which in the plan seems merely to peter out.

By January 1911, life had provided him with this correction. In February, he wrote to Heinemann's asking for the *Trespasser* manuscript to be returned, and added 'The third novel "Paul Morel", sticks where I left it four or five months ago, at the hundredth page. I've no heart to tackle a serious work just now' (I, 230). In fact he never took up this draft again; he started afresh, and the manuscript of this first version has disappeared.

He began the second version, 'Paul Morel II' as it is called, in March 1911, announcing to Louie Burrows 'I have begun Paul Morel again. I am afraid it will be a terrible novel. But, if I can keep it to my idea and feeling, it will be a great one' (I, 237). In a letter the following day to Helen Corke, saying that he had begun the novel again, he added '... glory, you should see it. The British public will stone me if ever it catches sight' (I, 239). The idea that it would be 'terrible' suggests that he had resolved to face the painful self-involvement; but the idea that the public would stone him suggests also that he was going to be frank about sexuality. He rapidly wrote some 350 pages between March and the summer, and again came to a halt. Much of this manuscript survives. It follows, in places, the original plan; so that it is still very different from the eventual novel. The most startling, indeed melo-dramatic, incident is where Walter Morel throws a carving-steel at his son Arthur, kills him, goes to prison and dies of remorse after his release. Something like this had actually happened in the household of Lawrence's uncle, except that the father had not been sent to prison; but this proof that life can be quite as strange as fiction does not make the incident anything but what French journalism calls a *fait divers* (Tragic incident in miner's home: Father kills son with thrown steel). Apart from that, the Miriam-figure has begun to take shape, and the conflict between her and the mother is beginning to be an important element. A Clara Dawes-figure has just been introduced by the end, and may reflect Lawrence's involvement with a married woman, Alice Dax.

His reports on the writing come mainly from letters to Louie. It is clear that he was writing painfully slowly, and without any zest; what kept him going was the thought that he had to finish in order to get money for them to be married on. But in any case the impulse that had led him to propose to Louie seemed increasingly to have been a mistake; he was fond of her, but not much more. That underlying consciousness may have been complicating his already mixed feelings about the work. He sent her a large batch of manuscript in late May, and came to a halt in July. We can infer a feeling that he had 'got it wrong' both in his writing and in his living. So in October he wrote to Louie 'I haven't done a stroke of Paul for months – don't want to touch it' (I, 310).

That same month, some instinct led him to get in touch with Jessie again. He made a complicated arrangement to meet her in London at a theatre with Helen Corke and his brother George. As a result of their conversation that evening, he sent her the manuscript, and she made a crucial intervention.

Of course, her account, written by the mature woman, and published in 1935, is at best a memorial reconstruction, and has elements of hindsight and self-justification. But she was a remarkable woman, and there is every reason to suppose she had been a remarkable girl. Her recollection of 'Laetitia', one of the early drafts of *The White Peacock* is shrewd, even mordant. One may wonder whether her lack of self-assurance, her love and her kindness had allowed her to say to Lawrence in 1906 what she says in her book, but she was capable, certainly, of seeing it. In 1911 she was older, had won a painful independence of Lawrence, had self-assurance and a great belief in his ultimate gift, and had no reason to be anything but frank. The draft now before her had some of the same weaknesses as the earlier writing, especially a kind of unreality which fell into sentimental excess. In both cases her word was 'story-bookish'. Here is her record:

He had written about two-thirds of the story, and seemed to have come to a standstill. The whole thing was somehow tied up. The characters were locked together in a frustrating bondage, and there seemed no way out. The writing oppressed me with a sense of strain.

It was extremely tired writing. I was sure that Lawrence had had to force himself to do it. The spontaneity that I had come to regard as the distinguishing feature of his writing was quite lacking. He was telling the story of his mother's married life, but the telling seemed to be at second hand, and lacked the living touch. I could not help feeling that his treatment of the theme was far behind the reality in vividness and dramatic strength. Now and again he seemed to strike a curious, half-apologetic note, bordering on the sentimental ... A nonconformist minister whose sermons the mother helped to compose was the foil to the brutal husband. He gave the boy Paul a box of paints, and the mother's heart glowed with pride as she saw her son's budding power ... It was story-bookish. The elder brother Ernest, whose short career had always seemed to me most moving and dramatic, was not there at all. I was amazed to find there was no mention of him. The character Lawrence called Miriam was in the story, but placed in a bourgeois setting, in the same family from which he later took the Alvina of *The Lost Girl*. He had placed Miriam in this household as a sort of foundling ...

The theme developed into the mother's opposition to Paul's love for Miriam. In this connection several remarks in this first draft impressed me particularly. Lawrence had written: 'What was it he (Paul Morel) wanted of her (Miriam)? Did he want her to break his mother down in him? Was that what he wanted?'

And again: 'Mrs Morel saw that if Miriam could only win her son's sex-sympathy there would be nothing left for her.'

In another place he said: 'Miriam looked upon Paul as a young man tied to his mother's apron-strings.' Finally, referring to the people around Miriam, he said: 'How should they understand her – petty trades-people!' But the issue was left quite unresolved. Lawrence had carried the situation to the point of deadlock and stopped there.

As I read through the manuscript I had before me all the time the vivid picture of the reality. I felt again the tenseness of the conflict, and the impending spiritual clash. So in my reply I told him I was very surprised that he had kept so far from reality in his story; that I thought what had really happened was much more poignant and interesting than the situations he had invented. In particular I was surprised that he had omitted the story of Ernest, which seemed to me vital enough to be worth telling as it actually happened. Finally I suggested that he should write the whole story again, and keep it true to life.

Two considerations prompted me to make these suggestions. First of all I felt that the theme, if treated adequately, had in it the stuff of a magnificent story. It only wanted setting down, and Lawrence possessed the miraculous power of translating the raw material into significant form. That was my first reaction to the problem. My deeper thought was that in the doing of it Lawrence might free himself from his strange obsession with his mother. I thought he might be able to work out the theme in the realm of spiritual reality, where alone it could be worked out, and so resolve the conflict in himself. Since he had elected to deal with the big and difficult subject of his family, and the interactions of the various relationships, I felt he ought to do it faithfully – 'with both hands earnestly,' as he was fond of quoting. It seemed to me that if he was able to treat the theme with strict integrity he would thereby walk into freedom, and cast off the trammelling past like an old skin. (ET 190–2)

There might be a self-interest there; if Lawrence could so free himself, might he not return to her? And since she was so good a critic (Louie had nothing to say) would he not always need her? However, the 'realm of spiritual reality' was not a place in which Lawrence could meet her, since he situated it elsewhere. And further, the notion of casting off the trammelling past like a snake-skin is an illusion. Lawrence might at that moment have shared it; writing to his former colleague Arthur McLeod in October 1913, he wrote 'I felt you had gone off from me a bit, because of *Sons and Lovers*. But one sheds ones sicknesses in books – repeats and presents again ones emotions, to be master of them' (*The Letters of D. H. Lawrence*, Vol. II, Cambridge, 1981, p. 90). That is a little less absolute; to be master of them is not the same as being free of them. The underlying metaphor in 'shed' may be of leaves rather than skins, but remains external.

'Significant form' is a Bloomsbury shibboleth of the 1920s, and Lawrence, in the 1920s, rejected it. But 'form' itself was becoming an issue; and the importance of Jessie's intervention is that she linked the question of form with that of catharsis and that of faithfulness to a lived experience. Only if he got the novel into the right form would he be free of his problem, and the right form, for her, would be a faithful record, 'true to life'. These are the other crucial aesthetic issues.

As it turned out, Jessie was storing up her own eventual disappointment by creating so firm an expectation that the final draft would be faithful to *her* recollection of what they had lived through together. Nonetheless, she had set Lawrence looking for a path that he had not instinctively found.

His fictions have two elements, broadly speaking: an element of the powerfully imagined, and one of the rendering of experience which he had himself seen or lived through. In his early writing, the purely imaginative element could lead him into a weak kind of romance; he needed the other to keep his world real. But the trouble then was, as he said to Jessie when he introduced the gamekeeper-figure Annable into *The White Peacock*, 'He *has* to be there ... He makes a sort of balance. Otherwise it's too much one thing, too much *me*' (ET 117).

Of course, the division 'imaginative/real' is unsustainable; the element of his own experience can only be a re-creation, and this too is imaginative. He needed to keep the two elements working on each other. But we have come already to the main critical issue posed for readers of *Sons and Lovers*, ever since Jessie Chambers, reading the penultimate draft, was shocked to see what he had done, felt herself betrayed and realised that it was not so simple after all to drop a past self like a skin. The issue is irresolvable insofar as the participants can have no objectivity, and we, the readers, cannot adjudicate from a knowledge of the facts other than the one the novel gives us. But we are led to the question: in dealing with their experience were his departures from 'fact' requirements of art, or were they failures of courage or self-knowledge? This turns naturally into technical questions: for instance, does the narrative voice identify itself too closely with Paul Morel? Inevitably, we must return to this.

Meanwhile, there is little doubt that Jessie's intervention was crucial. It had made Lawrence's way more clear to him, but he also knew more clearly how painful it was going to be. On 3 November 1911 he wrote to Louie: 'Tonight I am going to begin Paul Morel again, for the third and last time ... It is a book the thought of which weighs heavily upon me ... I really dread setting the pen to paper' (I, 321–2). He had reached page 74 of 'Paul Morel III' when he became seriously ill on 19 November. The pneumonia was like a physical expression of his year of grieving, and his sense of being in an emotional impasse, with his life as totally blocked as this attempt at a novel.

Following his story, one has the sense that 1912 was like a resurrection. After a convalescence in January at Bournemouth, he did three decisive things. He ended his engagement to Louie on 4 February, and resigned from his teaching post on 28 February. He was going to make a living as a writer; so in six weeks or so he revised *The Trespasser* for publication, using the notes on the first draft given him by Edward Garnett.

Garnett, an editor of genius, was like Hueffer a friendly and disinterested man. He was at the time reader for Duckworth, a 'coming' publisher, and he hoped eventually to attract the promising young author Lawrence to the firm. Like Hueffer, he had worked with Conrad; all three of them shared the reigning concept of 'form', derived ultimately from Flaubert. In the case of *The Trespasser*, Garnett had simply written letters and notes: but there must have been conversations as well, since Lawrence had stayed at Garnett's home in October. Hueffer too had talked to Lawrence about the book in his breezy way: he was the first person to tell Lawrence that of course he was a genius, but ... In this case, the book had every fault a Flaubertian could find, especially a failure to be 'impersonal', and was 'erotic' into the bargain. Lawrence absorbed as much of the criticism as he felt he needed, and revised the book swiftly, feeling a certain distance from it. He now needed to be published, because he had no means of support but his writing. *The Trespasser* finished, he thought he might be able to finish 'Paul Morel' in the seven weeks remaining before he planned to go to Germany to visit relatives. Perhaps he would write 'travel' pieces there.

Jessie had promised him some notes, which he collected in February; he then took up the story where it had been left off in November. He took sections of the book to Jessie as he wrote, and she returned these to him with comments, written on the manuscript and separate sheets – most of them in the sense that 'It wasn't like that', and some of them very passionately expressed. This repeated experience might have been a warning to her that Lawrence was writing a novel;

but she would have replied that there was an essential truth which a novel had to catch. When Lawrence got to the places where the conflict between Mrs Morel and Miriam was the central theme, he posted the pages to her, she later said, rather than face her with them.

For a man who had been mortally ill three months earlier, Lawrence's life was now lived as if he had the strength of ten. He had rewritten one book, and was rewriting another. In March he made a visit to Alice Dax and her husband in Shirebrook, and probably made love to her, not for the first but perhaps for the last time. Alice Dax, like Clara Dawes in the novel, was married, blonde, discontented – indeed a bit of a rebel, with intellectual interests which included suffragism. But Clara also owes something to Frieda Weekley, born von Richthofen, wife of one of Lawrence's professors at University College, Nottingham, also blonde, married and discontented – indeed a rebel of seismic quality. Her family were minor Prussian aristocrats; her father, an army officer, had a gambling habit, a mistress and, reputedly, a love-child. Her sisters formed marriages and liaisons with advanced intellectuals; and Frieda herself had had as lover Otto Gross, a charismatic but totally unstable pupil of Freud's, who had, as the expression goes, given her ideas. It was another world, another ethos.

Thinking to enlist Professor Weekley's advice on possible teaching in Germany, Lawrence called on him at his home, and fell in love with his wife. Her own reminiscence of the meeting at her home one Sunday morning, with her husband absent, tells how Lawrence immediately took her into his confidence about his emotional life and his failures with women. She, instead of offering the correct social response (quasi-motherly concern), intellectualised: they talked about Oedipus. It must have been enormously liberating for him to have his problem instantly converted from a personal conflict into a universal experience, and to talk to a person with no trace of conventionality. This too was in March, and another good reason for not calling on Jessie in person.

At the end of the month he delivered the last pages to Jessie, before going to visit his old friend George Neville in

Derbyshire. Her record is quite clear that she saw the ending at this time; for she felt hurt and bitter, indeed betrayed. Her extensive comment survives in her book, is inevitably an important document, and has been influential. It is essential to remember that it is based on the third draft of 'Paul Morel', very little of which survives. (On the other hand it is impossible to believe that when she came to write her own book so many years later, she had not read the published novel, even if she had earlier found it too painful. There is an inherent probability that her recollection of 'Paul Morel III' is complicated by a knowledge of *Sons and Lovers*, and without a clear sense of the differences between the two.)

She returned it to him on 1 April with some notes, but she was too upset to talk to him about it, and he was too defensive. On 3 April he told Garnett that he would finish 'this week − the first draft. It'll want a bit of revising. It's by far the best thing I've done' (I, 381). Does that mean that he intended to do something to meet Jessie's objections? In a week he could not do much; in any case the proofs of *The Trespasser* arrived, and had to be corrected quickly. On 11 April he told Walter de la Mare, then acting as Heinemann's reader: 'I have finished in its first form the colliery novel. Now I want to leave it for a month, when I shall go over it again. There are parts I want to change. Shall I send it to you for your opinion now at once, before I do any revising, or shall I put it close together before you see it? As you will' (I, 383).

Things now moved fast. On 21 April he said a last goodbye to Jessie, and on 3 May he left for Germany with Frieda, taking the manuscript with him. It was not at first clear to either of them that they were eloping, but in the next weeks this was decided. Somehow, Lawrence also managed to work on 'Paul Morel'. Jessie records a letter from him saying that he was 'going through *Paul Morel*. I am sorry it turned out as it has' (ET 216). Did he mean the novel, their love, both? On 24 May he and Frieda went to Icking, near Munich, staying there for two months. From this point one has to imagine the active influence of Frieda in daily conversation, working as a direct counterforce to any influence which Jessie could exert as a memory. On 10 June Lawrence wrote to de la Mare:

I sent that novel 'Paul Morel' off to William Heinemann yesterday. Now I know it's a good thing, even a bit great. It's different from your stuff ... It's not so strongly concentric as the fashionable folk under French influence − you see I suffered badly from Hueffer re Flaubert and perfection − want it. It may seem loose − and I may cut the childhood part − if you think better so − and perhaps you'll want me to spoil some of the good stuff. But it is rather great. (I, 416−17)

This, then, was 'Paul Morel III', completed. William Heinemann himself, presumably on the advice of de la Mare, rejected the book rapidly, writing on 1 July:

I have read PAUL MOREL with a good deal of interest and, frankly, with a good deal of disappointment, especially after what you wrote to me with regard to your feeling about the book and the view you took that it was your best work.

I feel that the book is unsatisfactory from several points of view; not only because it lacks unity, without which the reader's interest cannot be held, but more so because its want of reticence makes it unfit, I fear, altogether for publication in England as things are. The tyranny of the Libraries is such that a book far less out-spoken would certainly be damned (and there is practically no market for fiction outside of them).

In declining this manuscript, with many regrets, I would like to say that I am a great admirer of your writing, that certain parts in PAUL MOREL strike me as good as anything I have ever read of yours; but as whole it seems to me painfully mistaken, if for no other reason than that one has no sympathy for any character in the book. A writer must create interest in his characters. Even, after a while, one's interest in Paul flags, − while, in the early part, the degradation of his mother, supposed to be of gentler birth, is almost inconceivable. (I, 421, n.)

Heinemann was representing two views: his own commercial sense, as a publisher, that Lawrence's new work would offend public taste, especially as represented by the buyers for the circulating libraries, and would not therefore sell; and the views of his advisers, notably de la Mare, that the book was not good art, lacked 'form'. De la Mare expressed this rather loosely in a letter to Garnett: 'It seems to me to need pulling together: it is not of a piece. But the real theme of the story is not arrived at till half way through' (I, 424, n.). He had, like others later, failed to see how Part I foreshadows Part II; so a concern with 'form' can be a blindfold. Heinemann's point about 'character' was central to conventional thought about the novel at the time; and *now* we think of Lawrence as the writer who did more than any other to undermine facile notions about character. The point about the mother's 'degradation' shows that class consciousness was pervasive and prejudicial.

The shock presented by the 'want of reticence' was closely related; again, we now think of Lawrence as the writer who more than any other broke down this barrier. He had in 1910 found Heinemann squeamish about some mild physicalities in *The White Peacock*, anz had with mingled amusement and exasperation made some cuts in consequence. But he had been much more outspoken in *Sons and Lovers*, as the Cambridge text demonstrates: the passages later deleted by Garnett on sexual grounds and now reinstated were presumably like these passages or may even have been stubbornly carried forward from the text which Heinemann refused. The cuts do not greatly diminish the force of these scenes; they remained, even as originally published, undoubtedly the most explicit and the most engaged descriptions of sexual acts in the whole of English literature to that date; not comic as in Chaucer, not intellectually metaphorised as in Donne, and without the cheeky euphemisms of eighteenth-century smut or the double meanings and tactical suspension points of Sterne. Lawrence later recalled Heinemann saying that *Sons and Lovers* was the 'dirtiest' book he had ever read; and he had probably read some truly dirty books. What actually shocked, in Lawrence, was that he was not being 'dirty', which was an underground but understood pornographic convention. He was saying what could not so far be said at all, still less written, still less published and placed in libraries; and so going right through the wall of convention. Lawrence had had more than a refusal; he had had a warning of what in 1915 would descend on him with the banning of *The Rainbow*: the reaction, reinforced by the *Lady Chatterley's Lover* episode of 1928, which typecast him as a writer about, even obsessed with, sex.

He wrote instantly to Garnett, and poured out a set of part-wild, part-comic imprecations about his fellow-countrymen ('They've got white of egg in their veins, and their spunk is that watery its a marvel they can breed.') Garnett wrote back helpfully: on 4 July Lawrence sent him the manuscript, saying 'Anything that wants altering I will do'; and on 8 July 'It would be rather nice if you made a few notes again. I will squash the first part together – it is too long' (I, 422–3). Garnett probably thought he would now get the book for Duckworth, but there would have to be negotiations about its form and content. By 18 July Garnett had sent some notes; Lawrence said 'I agree with all you say', but went on, more warily: 'and will do all I can. I'll do my best' (I, 426). Further notes ('awfully nice and detailed') came on 22 July, with the manuscript. 'I *loathe* Paul Morel' the letter ends (I, 427); Lawrence must mean the character, reminder of a past self.

Garnett's notes are lost, but some preliminary jottings transcribed by the Barons (*SL*, xl–xli) give some hints: 'these pages no thankyou' – does that refer to a sexual encounter? And 'you are insensibly making Paul too much of a hero ... you identify your sympathies too much with Paul's wrath' was a shrewd pointer and might have produced the response about 'loathing' him.

Duckworth accepted the book for publication, explicitly or implicitly on the understanding that Garnett was going to guide it through in his usual helpful way, making himself answerable to the firm for its eventual acceptability. On the eve of his departure with Frieda on their memorable tramp through the Alps to Italy, Lawrence told Garnett 'I am going to write Paul Morel over again – it'll take me 3 months' (I, 430–1). He had already made a start on 'Paul Morel IV', reducing the first 85 pages to 76; but now sent the manuscript by train with his other luggage to Riva. He and Frieda reached the town in the first week of September; on the 7th he wrote to Garnett 'I am glad to be settling down, to get at that novel.

I am rather keen on it. I shall re-cast the first part altogether.'
In a postscript Frieda wrote:

I think L. quite missed the point in 'Paul Morel'. He really loved
his mother more than any body, even with his other women, real
love, sort of Oedipus, his mother must have been adorable − he is
writing P.M. again, reads bits to me and we fight like blazes over it,
he is so often beside the point ... (I, 449)

Lawrence had said something similar to Rachel Annand Taylor,
to Louie and to Jessie in December 1910; but had not perhaps
conveyed it in the novel until now. Arguing with Frieda may
have helped Lawrence to see what he wanted to say; one may
doubt whether this was often what she thought he ought
to say.

The prolonged stay on Lake Garda, the sense of being
settled with Frieda, above all perhaps the feeling of being
launched into a new life, away from Eastwood, his mother,
Jessie and the others − all this meant that Lawrence was now
in a position to look entirely afresh at 'Paul Morel'. On 17
September he wrote to McLeod, 'Paul Morel is *better* than
the *White Peacock* or *The Trespasser*. I'm inwardly very proud
of it, though I haven't yet licked it into form − am still at
that labour of love' (I, 455). That is a hint that 'form' was
not an idea he discounted altogether, but the old bear-cub
analogy suggests that something has to be born first, and
then is lovingly shaped by the parent. On 15 October, in a
letter to Garnett he suddenly suggested the present title: 'I have
done ³⁄₅ of Paul Morel. Can I call it *Sons and Lovers*?' (I, 462).
This in turn suggests that reworking the 'form' has caused
him to come on the deeper significance of the book; one can
read the sentence a few lines later as related to the 'bear-
cub' image: 'I've got a heap of warmth and blood and tissue
into that fuliginous novel of mine.'

Since so little of the previous draft survives, one can only
speculate how much Jessie's comments, Garnett's notes,
Frieda's suggestions and above all Lawrence's new thoughts
had altered the novel, but the Barons analyse the remaining
material (*SL*, xliii), concluding: 'By introducing a series of

such animated dialogues, Lawrence greatly elaborated the early years of William, the character based on his older brother, Ernest, whose life story Jessie Chambers had urged him to include.' This shift of emphasis gives Lawrence the plural nouns in his new title. The Barons also point out the extent to which the present chapter VII, 'Lad-and-Girl Love' was extended at this time: surely another attempt to meet Jessie's criticisms.

On 30 October he wrote to Garnett: 'I've done all but the last hundred or so pages ... and those I funk. But it'll be done easily in a fortnight ... Will *Sons and Lovers* do for a title? I've made the *book heaps* better − a million times' (I, 466). In her memoir, Frieda recalled that 'when he wrote his mother's death he was ill and his grief made me ill too' (*SL*, xliv): the Barons detect the stress in the handwriting in the manuscript. Nonetheless, on 19 November he could at last write to Garnett an important letter which in intention is not unlike the brief letter to de la Mare covering the previous draft but is now made long, explicit and formal. He tackles the London Flaubertians on their own ground; can they be made to see 'form' less externally? He had dropped a hint a week or so before; writing to Garnett about his own play *Jeanne d'Arc*, and hinting very tactfully that Garnett couldn't 'do' women, he had said 'No, I *don't* think you have a high opinion of women. They have got each an internal *form*, an internal self which remains firm and individual whatever love they may be subject to' (I, 470). Form as self: it redefines both words, especially if self is something which one grows into, sometimes through surprising transformations. And then, on 19 November:

I hasten to tell you I sent the MS. of the Paul Morel novel to Duckworth, registered, yesterday. And I want to defend it, quick. I wrote it again, pruning it and shaping it and filling it in. I tell you it has got form − *form*: haven't I made it patiently, out of sweat as well as blood. It follows this idea: a woman of character and refinement goes into the lower class, and has no satisfaction in her own life. She has had a passion for her husband, so the children are born of passion, and have heaps of vitality. But as her sons grow up she selects them as lovers − first the eldest, then the second. These sons are *urged* into life by their reciprocal love of their mother − urged

on and on. But when they come to manhood, they can't love, because
their mother is the strongest power in their lives, and holds them.
– It's rather like Goethe and his mother and Frau von Stein and
Christiana –. As soon as the young men come into contact with
women, there's a split. William gives his sex to a fribble, and his
mother holds his soul. But the split kills him, because he doesn't
know where he is. The next son gets a woman who fights for his
soul – fights his mother. The son loves the mother – all the sons
hate and are jealous of the father. The battle goes on between the
mother and the girl, with the son as object. The mother gradually
proves stronger, because of the tie of blood. The son decides to
leave his soul in his mother's hands, and, like his elder brother, go
for passion. He gets passion. Then the split begins to tell again.
But, almost unconsciously, the mother realises what is the matter,
and begins to die. The son casts off his mistress, attends to his mother dying.
He is left in the end naked of everything, with the drift towards
death.

It is a great tragedy, and I tell you I've written a great book.
It's the tragedy of thousands of young men in England – it may
even be Bunny's tragedy [David Garnett, Edward's son]. I think it
was Ruskin's, and men like him. – Now tell me if I haven't worked
out my theme, like life, but always my theme. Read my novel –
it's a great novel. If *you* can't see the development – which is slow
like growth – I can.

Then, some paragraphs later:

Have I made those naked scenes in Paul Morel tame enough. You
cut them if you like. Yet they are so clean – and I *have* patiently
and laboriously constructed that novel.

Frieda added a powerful and shrewd postscript, one of the
first and still one of the best pieces of Lawrence criticism:

I also feel as if I ought to say something about L.s formlessness.
I don't think he has 'no form'; I used to. But now I think anybody
must see in Paul Morel the hang of it. The mother is really the
thread, the domineering note, I think the honesty, the vividness
of the book suffers if you subject to it 'form'. I have heard so much
about 'form' with Ernst [her husband], why are you English so keen
on it, their form wants smashing in almost any direction, but they
cant come out of their snail house. I know it is so much safer. That's
what I love Lawrence for, that he is so plucky and honest in his
work, he dares to come out in the open and plants his stuff down
bald and naked, really he is the only revolutionary worthy of the
name, that I know, any new thing must find a new shape, then

afterwards one can call it 'art'. I hate art, it seems like grammar, wants to make a language all grammar, language was first and then they abstracted a grammar; I quite firmly believe that L is quite great in spite of his 'gaps'. Look at the vividness of his stuff, it knocks you down I think. It is perhaps too 'intimate' comes too close, but I believe that is youth and he has not done, not by long chalks! Dont think I am impudent to say all this, but I feel quite responsible for 'Paul'. I wrote little female bits and lived it over in my own heart. I am sure he is a real artist, the way things pour out of him, *he* seems only the pen, and isnt that how it ought to be? We *all* go for things, look at them with preconceived notions, things must have a 'precedence'. We have lost the faculty of seeing things unprejudiced, live off our own bat, think off our own free mind. Good gracious, what a tirade! (I, 476–9)

Garnett was no doubt thinking in terms of publication in the spring, supposing that the novel was ready to go ahead; but almost certainly he expected that there was an editing job to be done, and Lawrence's letter probably rang warning bells in his mind. He read fast, and reacted equally fast, and decisively. By 1 December Lawrence was writing:

I sit in sadness and grief after your letter. I daren't say anything. All right, take out what you think necessary – I suppose I shall see what you've done when the proofs come, at any rate. I'm sorry I've let you in for such a job – but don't scold me too hard, it makes me wither up.

D[uckworth]'s terms are quite gorgeous –

But I'm so afraid you'll repress me once more, I daren't say anything ...

Tell me anything considerable you are removing – (sounds like furniture). (I, 481–2)

Garnett's letter must have been a sort of sandwich: the filling was an offer of publication, with a good royalty and an advance of £100 on the day of publication (a year's starting salary as a schoolmaster; what he had hoped to save in order to marry Louie; and Italy was a much cheaper place to live in than England). The bread was a statement that there must be cuts, and furthermore that Garnett was now going to make them himself: no more helpful notes for Lawrence to consider. Worse still, Lawrence was not going to be consulted or shown the manuscript again; once cut, it was to go straight to the printer. Garnett wanted speed, and he wanted no argument: once the book was in proof, substantial reinstatement was impossible, and in the last resort Garnett would control that stage too, since the proofs would pass over his desk.

So far as Garnett was concerned, he was doing his day-to-day job, which included routine cutting of manuscripts to make books the right length for the right selling price, and cutting out also things which would lead to actual lawsuits or would simply put off the public, and especially the libraries. Publishers' contracts, then as now, contained a clause to the effect that the book shall contain nothing libellous or scandalous, or in breach of copyright; and editorial staff, then as now, kept an eye on this. Lawrence was a talented man, but his book was too long; and the 'want of reticence' was as marked as when Heinemann thought it 'the dirtiest book he had ever read'. The Barons summarise the changes as follows:

Garnett's editorial marks on the manuscript can be clearly identified. Although his main concern was to shorten considerably and to censor a little, it was inevitable that his choice of passages to delete would reflect his policy with regard to the novel's form; and accordingly they bulk large in the early chapters. Nearly all the reduction in length took place in chapters I to XI, and the censorship in chapters XI–XIII. There were no cuts in the last two chapters. In total he deleted eighty passages, varying from 2 to 185 lines, which shortened the manuscript by 2,050 lines, about a tenth ...

In chapter I Garnett deleted just over a hundred lines out of eleven hundred ... In chapter II he deleted about 250 out of approximately 900 lines ... But in chapter III ... Garnett removed several whole episodes in a total reduction of approximately 320 out of 750 lines. These were mainly scenes in the life of William, which serve to diversify William's role as a precedent for Paul ...

... Garnett took only one passage of nine lines out of chapter IV. Many of the passages he deleted in chapters V to X were dialogue, some were whole conversations ... The longest sequence Garnett cancelled was Lawrence's four-page description in chapter VIII of the regular weekly rendezvous between Paul and Miriam at the Bestwood library ...

Garnett's censorship was light. He removed six sentences from the most explicit scene in chapter XII ... one and a half from ... chapter XIII and a phrase from chapter XI ... Otherwise he censored single words ... But when checking the proofs Garnett extended his censorship of the same scenes ... (SL, xlix–l)

While waiting to see what Garnett had done, Lawrence allowed his feelings to escape in letters, especially to the artist Ernest Collings. Writing to him on 24 December, about art, he said 'The difficulty is to find exactly the form one's passion ... wants to take.' He goes on to say that his novel will be out in February, and then his irritation slips out: 'It's good of you to be only thirty. These damned old stagers want to train up a child in the way it should grow, whereas if it's destined to have a snub nose, it's sheer waste of time to harass the poor brat into Roman-nosedness. They want me to have form: that means, they want me to have *their* pernicious ossiferous skin-and-grief form, and I won't' (I, 491–2).

To Garnett he had to be more careful: in any case his feelings were genuinely mixed, and included liking, gratitude and hope of help to come. On 29 December he said 'I'm glad to hear you like the novel better. I don't much mind what you squash out' (I, 496). But on 12 January 1913 he wrote:

The thought of you pedgilling away at the novel frets me. Why can't I do those things? − I can't. I could do hack work, to a certain amount. But apply my creative self where it doesn't want to be applied, makes me feel I should bust or go cracked. I *couldn't* have done any more at that novel − at least for six months. I must go on producing, producing, and the stuff must come more and more to shape each year. But trim and garnish my stuff I cannot − it *must* go. (I, 501)

'Go' here means what he had said to Collings: 'I am a great admirer of my own stuff while it's new, but after a while I'm not so gone on it − like the true maternal instinct, that kicks off an offspring as soon as it can go on its own legs' (I, 491–2).

The proofs started to come; having returned the first batch of galleys, he wrote to Garnett on 18 February: 'It goes well, in print, don't you think? Don't you think I get people into my grip? You did the pruning jolly well, and I am grateful. I hope you'll live a long long time, to barber up my novels for me before they're published. I wish I weren't so profuse − or prolix, or whatever it is. But I shall get better' (I, 517). That is not exactly insincere, but it needs to be placed alongside the remarks to Collings, which represent his real feelings.

Lawrence may be saying that as long as he has to submit to
external judgements, he hopes it is going to be Garnett who
exercises them. But even Garnett would make nothing of the
work which Lawrence was at that moment engaged on – the
projected novel which turned into *The Rainbow* and *Women
in Love*; and Lawrence's trials with them made the difficulties
with *Sons and Lovers* look almost trivial.

Having returned all the galleys, Lawrence wrote to Garnett:
'It is rather a good novel – but if anything a bit difficult
to grasp as a whole, at first. Yet it *is* a unified whole, and I
hate the dodge of putting a thick black line round the figures
to throw out the composition ...' (I, 522). But it turned out
that a second proof was necessary; it seemed that someone
at Duckworth was anxious about the novel's 'want of reticence'
and Garnett had to prune a little more. Meanwhile Lawrence
had been served with papers for Frieda's divorce, and had
probably realised that he would be liable for costs; he needed
the advance on royalties even more: hence perhaps the exasper-
ated tone of his letter to Garnett of 11 March: 'I've got the
pip horribly at present. I don't mind if Duckworth crosses
out a hundred shady pages in *Sons and Lovers*. It's got to
sell, I've got to live' (I, 526).

There followed a sad last exchange with Jessie, who had
received a copy of Lawrence's *Love Poems*, just published,
and had written to thank him. He now sent her proofs of the
novel: 'I think you ought to see it before it's published ...
Frieda and I discuss you endlessly' (I, 527–8). She was too
hurt and offended to do more than 'glance' at a few pages,
so she was not in a position to discover what, if anything,
he had done to meet her own earlier criticism. She returned
his letter to him as a gesture of repudiation, and sent the
proofs on to his sister Ada (ET 218–20).

She had since they last communicated written a novel of
her own, first drafted as a short story and shown to Lawrence
in 1911. It had been even then a self-justification, and an
attempt to make him see things more from her point of view.
She called the novel 'The Rathe [early] Primrose' ('... which
forsaken dies', in Milton's *Lycidas*) and gave herself the

pseudonym Eunice Temple (hence the E.T. of her later *Personal Record* of Lawrence). She showed it Hueffer, whom she had met, and then to Garnett, and he in turn showed it to Lawrence in May. Hurt by having his letter returned, Lawrence was at first sardonic about her; when he actually read the novel he wrote: 'I should scarcely recognise her — she never used to *say* anything. But it isn't bad, and it made me so miserable I had hardly the energy to walk out of the house for two days' (I, 551). That first sentence provokes a good deal of thought about the relationship. Frieda too was touched: 'Miriam's novel is very lovable, I think, and one does feel so sorry for her, but it's a faded photograph of *Sons and Lovers*, she has never understood anything out of herself, no inner activity, but she does make one ache! I only just realised the amazing brutality of *Sons and Lovers*' (I, 550). Jessie's novel was not published, and she later destroyed it.

Meanwhile there had been a debacle about the dust-jacket of the novel; Duckworth had wanted a picture of a colliery on the front to emphasise the working-class setting, and Lawrence had tried to get the commission for Collings. In the end there was no picture, but it may be that Lawrence wrote or drafted the selling-copy: 'Mr. D. H. Lawrence's new novel covers a wide field: life in a colliery, on a farm, in a manufacturing centre. It is concerned with the contrasted outlook on life of two generations. The title, "Sons and Lovers," indicates the conflicting claims of a young man's mother and sweetheart for predominance.'

The book was published at last on 29 May 1913, in the text which Garnett had established. It was published in the USA in September by Mitchell Kennerley. For nearly eighty years, Lawrence's most popular novel was read in the form given to it by Edward Garnett, until *Sons and Lovers* was restored to its original form in the Cambridge edition of 1992. Fortunately the manuscript survived; Frieda gave it to Mabel Dodge Luhan in 1924, in return for the ranch in New Mexico which became the Lawrences' home; and eventually it was bought by the Library of the University of California at Berkeley.

I propose to show that by not recognising a structure that was, by the time Lawrence had finished the book, deeply considered, Garnett damaged an actual form without instating an equally considered new one, still less a better one. As for the idea of 'form' in the English novel in the first decade of the century, the ultimate source of this group of precepts was the letters of Flaubert. Here he told his correspondents what he was aiming at in his long struggles to bring his novels, especially *Madame Bovary*, to perfection. This took years, and the main difference between Flaubert and Lawrence is not so much in the form itself as in the verbalisation, the extreme consciousness of Flaubert's pursuit, as compared with Lawrence's habit of diving back into the pool of spontaneity.

Flaubert's pupil Maupassant wrote some incisive critical pieces which hardened the doctrine, and there was a conveniently short poem by Gautier, 'L'Art', which provided some analogies. The general sense that at this time the French were more sophisticated about art, especially the art of the novel, was conveyed by intermediaries. Walter Pater's article on 'Style' was published in 1888 and collected in *Appreciations* in 1895; it made much of Flaubert as the hero and saint of painful perfection, and used some of Gautier's analogies, especially those of the gem-cutter and the sculptor: art is a matter of cutting away redundancies, blowing away the last grains of dust to reveal the perfect form and surface. This is an external and facile view.

Henry James's critical essays included 'The Art of Fiction' in 1884, 'Guy de Maupassant' in 1888, and two brilliant essays on Flaubert, in 1893 and 1902. James's criticism was full, considered and in places sardonic; neither Maupassant nor Flaubert were presented as mere culture-heroes; but that is what they had become by now in common literary estimation. It should have been cautionary that James told the story of the first, serial, publication of *Madame Bovary*. Flaubert's old friend Maxime du Camp had become editor of the *Revue de Paris*; he had the honour of publishing the novel, but had on the eve of publication sent Flaubert a letter of 'advice and remonstrance'. 'This incomparable effusion, with its amazing reference to excisions and its suggestion that the work be placed in the hands of an expert and inexpensive corrector who will prepare it for publication' can be thought of as like Garnett's letters to Lawrence, equally practical, well-meant and misplaced.

Importantly for Lawrence, both Garnett and Hueffer had collaborated with Conrad, whose profound and at first incoherent genius, seeking expression, reached for the French predecessors as a kind of crutch. There are not only literal renderings of French originals conveyed into the texture of Conrad's novels; there was a pervasive, almost desperate sense that he had to follow Flaubert's precepts. Hueffer collaborated on two of the novels, and he and Conrad had long conversations in which they vied with each other in their admiration of, and their knowledge of, the French masters.

In the general literary consciousness, this orientation produced a vulgar aesthetic of the kind every age has, an unwritten rule-book. Every element of a novel must be subjected to a governing intention. Flaubert had talked about 'plan': the trouble with the English, he said, is that they lacked plan. If you replied that Dickens's enormous and complex plots, where everything is tied up at the end, showed, if anything, too much plan, you would be told that 'plot' is not the same thing at all. Plot had been too much depended on: 'plan', or the governing intention, sees rather that every element of the novel, and especially the imagery, coheres and combines to produce a unity of total effect. The great vice is redundancy; nothing must be superfluous. This insistence that there could be nothing gratuitous (not at all the same thing as redundancy) tended to shut out the spontaneous and the sense of life. Furthermore, the novelist must be 'impersonal'. What Flaubert had objected to originally was the habit of addressing the reader, still more that of telling the reader one's own opinion. The doctrine prevailed at a time when authorial manner or style (think of Henry James or Conrad) was at its most idiosyncratic, even though the novelist adopted devices such as an intervening narrator. It is no less odd that the savage irony, the self-laceration, of Flaubert and the often coarse situational sarcasm of Maupassant were thought 'impersonal', but that sort of blindness is induced by a conventional view.

This general aesthetic was pressed on Lawrence in conversation by those who could not see what he was doing. There was an element of pious lipservice in Hueffer's position; he wrote eighty-one books in a life which was not long; so the doctrine was more honoured in the breach than in the observance. As for Garnett, he was a working editor, doing the useful, the sensible thing in the time available; and when it came to the push the canons of Flaubert were only one of the operative considerations. The cut *Sons and Lovers* is shorter, but not for that reason more Flaubertian, than the original; rather the opposite, since Lawrence's final form bore a demonstrable relation to the canons.

Not that this was evident to the best judges of the time. Henry James had written an important essay for *The International Library of Famous Literature* (1899), that series of twenty volumes edited by Edward Garnett's father, which the Lawrence family owned, and in which Lawrence found his first introduction to many authors. The main point of James's essay was that the English novel should widen its view, its concerns, and above all it should cease to be so timid in its treatment of the sexual relationship. Yet in 1914, in 'The New Novel', a survey article written for *The Times Literary Supplement*, James failed to see that Lawrence had done what he had himself desiderated, failed because he was blinded by his own adherence to the old aesthetic. He could not find in *Sons and Lovers* 'the centre of interest' and 'the sense of the whole' − things he had failed to find in *War and Peace*, as it happened. Only in Compton Mackenzie did he find 'a controlling idea and a pointed intention'. It is a sad irony that the best of the older generation should fail to recognise the best of the new one.

Chapter 2

Form: narrative structure

Asked why they enjoyed *Sons and Lovers* and remember it with pleasure, many readers would answer that they found it vivid, or 'realistic'. This lifelikeness starts with the evocation of the countryside and the town, the mining-community and its people, and the Morel parents themselves, who are portrayed so carefully, so much in the round that most people find that good balances bad. We find fresh and arresting the scene where Morel gets up, breakfasts and goes off to the pit: this is how it once was, and it both renders a way of life, now lost, in a given place at a certain time, and gives us a sympathetic sense of him as a man comfortably rooted in his way of life and his work. What he is feeling at this moment, or as he picks mushrooms on the way to the pit (cut by Garnett) is the joy that is often unconscious. This is not wage slavery or industrial oppression; Morel lives in a way that he loves. What he does, where he lives, give him his identity. It is his emotional life which threatens it: just the opposite of the conventional notion of industrial life. Similarly the later scenes in which he does little cobbling or tinkering jobs about the house, makes fuses, or tells the children about 'down pit' show a man at ease with himself and his children, happy for the moment just to be, so that one is bound to ponder what has gone wrong.

A parallel with Morel's life at the pit is young Paul's introduction to work at Jordan's: the whole long day, from the train journey in to the return at night. The people at the little factory are realised in all their strange individuality; the organisation, the work, give the sense of a microcosm full of living energies. Day-to-day clerical work, writing letters, keeping accounts, sending out goods to customers, is what hundreds of millions still do, but does not get much of a showing in art.

I doubt if there is a more vivid rendering in literature of that world of daily work, seen in its fullness by someone who has done it.

Two brief quotations sum up this capacity to see ordinary things freshly. They show that 'realism' is an inadequate word. Paul goes to Jordan's for his interview with his mother: it is a strange new world: 'On the table was a pile of trusses, yellow wash-leather hoops tangled together. They looked new and living' (119). Some pages later, again with her, he looks down on his own world, and finds the same sense in it:

On the fallow land the young wheat shone silkily. Minton pit waved its plumes of white steam, coughed and rattled hoarsely ...
    'The world is a wonderful place,' she said, 'and wonderfully beautiful.'
    'And so's the pit,' he said. 'Look how it heaps together, like something alive, almost − a big creature that you don't know.' (152)

One remembers also Mrs Morel at the market, allowing herself to buy a pretty dish with cornflowers on it, and softening to the man she has got a bargain from; or standing, seeming to listen to her iron, or the noise her needle makes, sewing. These scenes balance the others in which Morel comes home late and drunk, and they quarrel.

Much of the writing seems to have this effortless lucid veracity, like Tolstoy's, so that scenes and people come up off the page like life. There are elements which are pure realism, creating the circumstances: little episodes like the yeast-seller 'Barm-O' (cut by Garnett), or 'Hose', the middleman who gets the miners' wives to seam stockings at twopence-halfpenny the dozen, or the way the wives, when the baby is coming, summon help from the woman next door: about 'raking' the fire at night and putting out the miner's pit-clothes to warm − the reader will reel off other examples once this game is started. There is too the serious social or industrial history; one learns what a butty is, how the mining teams work, what was paid and how it was divided up (the scene in which Paul collects his father's wages), how the wives managed in good weeks and bad including accidents and sickness, the hierarchy of streets to live in, and how the ashpits spoiled them all.

dialect

There is also the dialect, transcribed carefully and uncondescendingly, not quite for the first time in literature, since Jefferies' *Amaryllis at the Fair* had rendered a Southern dialect with equal care. But it is still a new note: this is dialect rendered by a speaker, not an observer; and while it is full of wit, savour and character it is not a way of demoting the speakers to a lower class in the drama, a kind of chorus with a tone of automatic comedy, as in Dickens, or even in Hardy. It is structural: Morel cannot speak any other way, except in parody, and his wife will not speak that way; it is an emblem of the rift between them. Paul can move in and out of dialect: with his mother and Miriam he speaks the language of consciousness: dialect is the language of instinctive tenderness in which he addresses Clara after they have made love for the first time. Genteel readers in 1913 might also have been shocked to read Baxter Dawes's bad language – presumably the first uses of 'bugger' and 'sod' in modern literature.

childhood

Then one thinks, these pleasures of fresh outward-looking are nearly all in Part I. This is not the eye of childhood, exactly, but childhood memories recovered with their persistent power and vividness. Or it is like being happily in love: the whole world comes alive in the same way. Part II is different; the presiding mood is bafflement, struggle, failure to get things clear, as in a frustration-dream. Something here is less impersonal: not more involved in what is related, but less able to stand outside and just see all round it. That something is the presiding consciousness. So far as it is Paul Morel's, it is in the nature of the case that it cannot be outside itself and objective. So far as it is Lawrence's, it cannot afford to be outside Paul's consciousness, giving the reader an undermining comment on what happens. It is Lawrence's intention that we should feel with his alter ego, enter into his state. How can he and we do this, and still remain free? It is the question.

Nearly all discussion of *Sons and Lovers* is conditioned by this knowledge that the book is based on Lawrence's own experience. The unsophisticated but sensible question, what is the novel about? is thus foreclosed: it is about his problems,

and the argument goes off into other questions such as, was
Lawrence fair to his parents or to Jessie? Even the after-
thought 'But this is a novel, not an autobiography' can be
diverted in the same direction by asking: does the narrative
voice seem too much Lawrence's, and is it too favourable
to Paul? The assumption is that we are dealing with fiction
as catharsis, as self-therapy. From early days, some readers
recognised an archetypal situation: here was Freud's Oedipal
conflict dramatised, in the longest and most vivid of all case-
histories, recorded by a self-analyst of genius. The implication
is the one reached long ago by Jessie: once Lawrence had
had this settling of accounts with himself and his family
situation he could go on to write what he really wanted to
write; and *Sons and Lovers* is therefore set aside from the
rest of the work. This begs the question, did he settle the
account, *could* he?

Lawrence himself seemed to foster this argument by making
remarks like the ones in the letter to McLeod (p. 22 above)
about 'shedding' his 'sickness'. A later reflection introduces
a slight shift of stance, but encourages us to stay within the
biographical frame: 'I should write a different *Sons and
Lovers* now. My mother was wrong, and I thought she was
absolutely right.' Similarly, in 'Women Are So Cocksure'
he wrote: 'My mother spoilt her life with her moral frenzy
against John Barleycorn ... And at fifty, when the best part
of life was gone, she realized it. And then what would she
not have given to have her life again, her young children,
her tipsy husband, and a proper natural insouciance, to get
the best out of it all' (*Phoenix*, ed. E. McDonald, 1936, p. 168).
The reader who bears in mind Lawrence's own dictum 'Never
trust the teller, trust the tale' might reply that the tale tells
us that it is not in the Mrs Morel he has given us to have that
reaction. But in any case the novel does both of the parent-
figures far more justice than he suggests.

The general instinct that this is importantly Lawrence's story
is not mistaken, provided that we see how much he has shaped
it in order to give it representative force, such that it ceases

to be merely personal; and how by doing so he has convincingly become impersonal without providing undermining comment.

This could not simply be a matter of doing what any writer might do in order to disguise the real people who are the originals of certain characters, or just to make a shapely plot. So, for instance, Paul is an artist, not a writer. It is the brother Arthur who goes to Nottingham High School and on to college, not Paul; indeed Paul's brothers and sisters are unlike Lawrence's in many ways, including their actual number. Lawrence only worked at Haywood's, the medical appliance manufacturers, for four months, whereas Paul works at Jordan's for years and becomes an overseer. Miriam is less of an intellectual than Jessie was; but then Paul is less of an intellectual than Lawrence. The whole affair with Clara Dawes, and the relationship of rivalry with her husband, is imagined, though it may borrow elements of Lawrence's affairs with Alice Dax and Frieda. And so on; one could specify smaller departures, and there must be thousands that we simply do not know about.

In one sense this *is* mere detail; the central story remains Lawrence's, and above all the conflict between his roles as son and as lover. Yet cumulatively, the differences begin to translate the story of Lawrence's childhood and youth into something wider. They should be seen as the detail of a larger change, where Lawrence's rewritings finally translated his material into 'form', to use the contentious term. This form does create an imaginative but dispassionate element in the writing, in the first place by creating noticeable parallels, symmetries and recurrences. These suggest that the central experience which is Paul's is part of a wider pattern, first within the family itself, then in the vividly created mining community, where it is a recognisable element of social morality, and finally in the whole universe which the closing paragraphs confront in all seriousness.

At two points especially all the themes coalesce: at the end of each Part. It is striking that the division into two Parts survives from the earliest 'plotting out'. The proportions are important; Part I has six chapters or some 160 pages, Part II eight or 280; the one is like a first movement preluding the other in which things are substantially developed and worked out. At the end of the first, the elder brother William, who is the central childish consciousness in the first three chapters, and whose experiences importantly prefigure Paul's, dies. Paul has now to move forward to claim his mother's attention. The little touch which the reader is most likely to notice as a link with the end of Part II is that as the father Morel and his mates struggle to bring the great coffin into the house the living child makes a claim, breaking into the Biblical note of the mother's grief:

> 'Oh my son – my son – my son!'
> 'Mother!' Paul whimpered, his hand round her waist. 'Mother!' She did not hear.
> 'Oh my son, my son!' she repeated. (169)

Two pages later, Paul is mortally ill, and the mother is forced to turn her attention to the living son, for fear that he too may die:

> 'I s'll die, mother!' he cried, heaving for breath on the pillow.
> She lifted him up, crying in a small voice:
> 'Oh, my son, my son!'
> That brought him to. He realised her. (171)

The transference has been made, for good and ill ('Mrs Morel's life now rooted itself in Paul'). At the end of Part II, in an enormous climax to the whole book, the son's first desperate claim, the one made as the coffin comes in, is repeated in exactly the same words, but he cannot now receive the later confirming answer. 'He realised her' had been, we have learned, a doubtful way of finding his own identity. Now he has to realise himself:

> 'Mother!' he whimpered, 'mother!'
> She was the only thing that held him up, himself, amid all this. And she was gone, intermingled herself! He wanted her to touch him, have him alongside with her.
> But no, he would not give in. (464)

The first edition and most subsequent printings misread 'whimpered' as 'whispered', thus eliminating a main clue to the parallel. It is like a musical motif recurring at important moments: here, at the end of each of the two large movements or acts. The reader is made to think of the parallels, but also of the differences in the situations: especially that the mother is now dead and the living son must either die or live as his own centre of life. The question is, has she enabled him, or has she incapacitated him? Can he become himself? The strange but powerful realism of 'He wanted her to touch him, have him alongside with her' starts as evocation of their being in bed together all those years ago. But it is equivocal now; a grown man can't want to be in bed with his mother. In any case, her bed is the grave. Does he want that? He realises that he does not.

Once that deft symmetry between the parts is recognised, other symmetries multiply. They become what Garnett called form or we now call structure; but they are not fully separable from what is also called style, the language, which occupies the next section of this study. So, for instance, in that extraordinary scene of William's homecoming, dead, the reader may feel the resonance of certain phrases which are also waiting, as it were, to become fully, orchestrally, deployed at the end of the book. I analyse that great finale below. Meanwhile, the waiting phrases are: 'The ash-tree stood monstrous and black, in front of the wide darkness'; 'the front door, which opened straight from the night into the room'; and 'by the open door, against the night, Annie stood leaning forward ...' (168–9). The ash-tree, resonating in the wind, has been established as a kind of link between the parents' discord and the night outside. The other phrases imply that as the huge coffin ('the great, dark weight') bursts in, 'night' and 'darkness' threaten to invade the home. They hint at more than death. These forces have been invoked earlier in the narrative, and are the elements which link what is personal with what is familial and what is universal, what is enormously out there. They are, here as elsewhere, dreads; and they raise the question, are they Paul's childish dreads, or Lawrence's, or is he, through Paul, putting us in touch with something universal to which the child-mind is open, and which we need to recover and respect?

Some of the recurrences are all-pervasive, a matter of the texture of the writing, which is usually metaphorical even when it seems to be realistic: I touch on these below: the ash-tree, the sense of night, of darkness, of a space waiting to burst in are examples. The structural ones may be duple, as between the two Parts: we have just seen the final one. Some are triple, reflecting the other structural principle that Paul has three women – his mother, Miriam and Clara – and Lawrence needs to inflect his motifs to represent the differing nature of the three relationships. Some of these recurrences are slight, almost unnoticeable: for instance Paul pins flowers, or berries, on to the breast of each of his three women (210, 281, 364); or he helps each of them over a stile (153, 184–5, 352). Each little incident is symptomatic, and expresses the nature of the woman and the relationship. So, for instance, Paul doesn't want his mother to know that he has pinned the flowers so carefully for Miriam, and breaks off, hearing her approach. Mrs Morel finds stiles a nuisance but doggedly goes over, refusing his help. Miriam is afraid to jump into his waiting arms (we think of the episodes with the pecking hen, and the swing, where she is also afraid to let herself go). Clara jumps wholeheartedly, laughing, and is caught and covered with kisses.

As for the duple pattern, that of the two sons, it is the simplest and most explicit – more so now that Garnett's cuts have been restored. In chapter I the baby which Gertrude Morel is carrying is Paul, but the child in whom she invests her hope is William ('The world seemed a dreary place ... at least until William grew up', 13). She has turned from the father; a crucial moment in the process is the hair-cutting episode (23–4; it is easy to think that Paul is the victim, but it is William). By the time Paul is born, 'Already William was a lover to her' and 'did not like the new baby' (44; cut by Garnett). William is antagonistic to the father long before Paul can be; 'all his young soul was his mother's' (49). The antagonism, the rivalry, shows itself most clearly in the scene when father and son nearly fight in the presence of the mother (83); there is a precise parallel in Part II where Paul also nearly fights with Morel (253). This follows a virtual love-scene between mother and son, which Morel interrupts; after the near-fight Paul begs his mother not to share the husband's bed. So the parallel is also a development, an intensification; once William is dead the mother turns to the chosen son, and he to her, with tragic force.

As William grows up, he shows himself clever and ambitious; in a long passage also cut by Garnett, he teaches other boys his skills, but is so much quicker than they are that he has no patience, and abuses them verbally (71). His mother has to remonstrate, in exactly the same way as, later, Mrs Leivers has to tell Paul to be more patient with Miriam (188–9). In the first passage, with William, there is a long quasi-courtship scene of loving play between mother and son, ending 'They left each other glowing warm: he made her feel warm inside, and she him' (73; cut). This is parallelled in Part II by more than one scene between Paul and his mother. There are well-imagined complexities here: for instance, in the scene where William puts on his Highlander's kit to go to a fancy-dress ball, 'all his pride was built on *her* seeing him' (76; also cut); but she refuses to look. It is conveyed to the reader that William has now displaced his father in a specific way, as skilful dancer. It was important in his courtship that Morel had had this gift (which Lawrence valued). It was part of the vitality which first won the mother's love, a matter in which he was a more favoured nature; so now the mother fears the boy will become like his father, while the father, remembering his own past skill and his pleasure in it, is obscurely jealous. These are scenes of some subtlety, but Garnett presumably failed to see the points being implied.

William's charm and grace mean that he is a favourite with the girls, and this makes his mother jealous; she turns the girls away at the door. 'And tell your girls, my son, that when they're running after you, they're not to come and ask your mother for you' she says (75). There are several implications here: the charm foreshadows Paul's gift with the girls at Jordan's, but the jealousy foreshadows the triangle with Paul and Miriam. But Mrs Morel's emotions are not merely negative:

... the carelessness went out of his eyes.

His mother ... felt a little chill at her heart. Was he going to 'come off'? ... Perhaps she only wanted him to be himself, to develop and bring to fruit all that she had put into him. In him, she wanted to see her life's fruition ... And with all the strength of her soul she tried to keep him strong and balanced and moving straight forwards. But he was baffling, without clarity of purpose. Sometimes he lapsed and was purely like his father ...

... She did not mind flirtations ... But she dreaded lest he should come a cropper over some shallow hussy. (77–8; cut by Garnett)

He says that the flirtations are nothing serious; and 'I shan't get married till I meet a woman like you' (74; cut). This is a painful irony; but it also foreshadows the several occasions when Paul makes exactly the same promise: Paul's later formulation, and the irony is now a savage one, is: 'I'll never marry while I've got you' (286). And of course he does not; the question at the end is, can he ever? In all these cases until the final one, both son–lovers indulge a little fantasy; the assumption is that Morel is dead, and mother and son are going to live together in a nice little house with a servant, and be happy ever after.

Her dread is fulfilled; William does 'come a cropper over some shallow hussy'. Here is one of the points where the duple pattern modulates into the triple one. William falls for his 'Gipsy', and brings her home, as Paul later brings Clara home: the symmetry is marked by Morel's being charming, indeed courtly, to both his sons' young women. Gipsy is pathetically inadequate beneath the glamour. Yet Paul too is captivated; and in a strange scene threads flowers in her hair, calling her a 'young witch-woman' (158); this parallels the later scene when he drops flowers over Clara's hair, saying 'Ashes to ashes and dust to dust/If the Lord won't have you the devil must' (279). Between the two incidents he has said to Miriam 'If you put red berries in your hair ... why would you look like some witch or priestess, and never like a reveller' (226). These are small examples of the peculiarly Lawrentian way of opening up the story towards another realm beyond social or psychological realism. Making sense of them here, one might point to the pervasive sense of a strange realm of 'night': here it is the place where witches, priestesses and revellers have their being. For a child, certainly; but for an adult?

Gipsy's photograph, in evening dress with naked shoulders, shocks Mrs Morel (126). Here is a reveller, a night-person, who has bewitched her son. 'When I'm with her in the evenings, I am awfully fond of her', he says (148), as if this explained something. (This note recurs with Paul and Clara.) In the day, she is trivial and useless, no companion. Mrs Morel has a specific fear, that William will be trapped into marriage; so she will not go to bed before the two young people have gone up separately ('Can't you trust us, mother?' he says, twice; 148). This is exactly like Paul and Clara later, after the theatre, fencing with *her* mother; but Paul eludes her watchfulness, to enter into the paradisal scene of love-making in the little Nottingham house when the old woman has gone up to bed (382ff). Mrs Morel's foreboding ('They'll hang on to each other till they kill each other', 164; cut) comes partly true; William's own prophecy wholly true ('He hated her ... "If I died, she'd have forgotten me in three months"', 163).

William dies of erysipelas, made fatal by overwork. Or that is the ordinary explanation of his death in Part I. In Part II Paul gives the death its deeper significance within the scheme of the whole novel. From a cosmic or Darwinian point of view it was mere 'waste'; his own insight is that it followed a tragic failure to follow the right path. In a long conversation with Miriam, cut by Garnett, he says 'I reckon we've got a proper way to go — and if we go it, we're all right ... But if we go wrong, we die. I'm sure our William went wrong somewhere ... What we are inside makes us so that we ought to go one particular way, and no other.' It does not occur to him that William 'went wrong' partly because of the relationship with his mother, so that there is a lesson for him; and this unconsciousness is dangerous. At this moment he has a sublime confidence that he himself is following his true course: 'Yes — I'm certain' (193). He has no sense yet that he is under the same spell, or in the same difficulty, as his brother. That hubris is profoundly questioned at the

end of the book, where he, like William, is left with the 'drift
... towards death' (451).

William's 'going wrong' is what his mother fears, though
she puts it in a way which Lawrence implicitly questions: in
the social—moral terms of her class. Here is one point where
the personal becomes the familial and the social in an external
way, and Lawrence builds it up in order to break it down. Mrs
Morel has 'gone wrong' herself through a mistaken marriage.
The fear that her sons will do the same leads her into a double
bind. Her jealousy, her fear of losing the two sons in whom
she has placed all her love, is reinforced by her sense that she
has invested her own fulfilment in them, and does not want
them to fail in life. That wish reinforces the prudent vigilance
of the parent who has to enforce the morality of the tribe —
if only to stop the children making the mistake she made.
William says of his first girls, 'I only want a bit of fun with
them'; she replies, 'But they don't merely want a bit of fun
with *you*' (74). She produces a startling dog-analogy, saying
that he presses up against girls wanting to be petted. He thinks
he can turn the figure against her: 'When they've done, I trot
away.' She replies, 'But one day you'll find a string round
your neck' (80). Dogs mate, but don't get married; they trot
away. William thinks they are free, but she reminds him that
they are domesticated, like it or not. She speaks as one who
is not free.

One book which Lawrence pondered on this topic was
Hardy's *Jude the Obscure*. Jude finds a string round his neck
when he is tricked into marriage by a girl who falsely tells
him she is pregnant. He does the right thing, by the standards
of the tribe, and the marriage is a disaster. William several
times insists to his mother that although he is clear that his
Gipsy is a 'fribble' (Lawrence's word in the letter to Garnett
about form) he has 'gone too far' to abandon her now; more
than once he says 'it' or 'he' has gone too far (161, 162).
'For *some* things, I couldn't do without her — .' What could
they be? 'I can't give her up *now*' (162). It is a shock to realise
that these coded messages may be the language of sexuality,
which was not allowed other language then. We infer that

he may have been seduced by her flagrant sexual display, and the code will not let him abandon a woman he has 'ruined'. It is a fatal weakness which Paul later refuses to emulate; twice he transgresses the tribal sexual rule; nonetheless it is clear to him when he breaks with Miriam, after she has given herself to him at his own insistence, that he has by the standards of their class, or indeed by any standards, done her a wrong. 'He knew he had landed her in a nasty hole, and was leaving her in the lurch' (340). He is returning her to her people, 'ruined' in the terms of the old morality which he can neither accept nor ignore:

As she went home, solitary, in her new frock, having her people to face at the other end, he stood still with shame and pain in the highroad, thinking of the suffering he caused her. (343)

Within his own family he has also had the example of his other brother Arthur. Leaving the army, he gets a girl pregnant, has to marry her, and the baby is born six months after the wedding:

He was caught now. It did not matter how he kicked and struggled, he was fast. For a time he chafed ... He grumbled for hours to his mother. She only said 'Well, my lad, you did it yourself, now you must make the best of it.' And then the grit came out in him. He ... acknowledged that he belonged to his wife and child, and did make a good best of it. (300−1)

That last phrase recurs a few pages later. Sue, the overseer at Jordan's, is leaving to get married, and says to Paul that she wishes she wasn't. Their little exchange shows how deeply the social-linguistic code is internalised.

'Nay Susan, you won't make me believe that.'
'Shan't I? You *can* believe it though. I'd rather stop here a thousand times.'
Paul was perturbed.
'Why, Susan?'
The girl's colour was high, and her eyes flashed.
'That's why!'
'And must you?'
For answer, she looked at him ... He understood.
'Ah, I'm sorry,' he said. Tears came to her eyes.

'But you'll see it'll turn out all right. You'll make the best of it,' he continued, rather wistfully.

'There's nothing else for it.'

'Yea, there's making the worst of it. Try and make it all right.'

(304–5)

'Making the best', or worst, of the shotgun wedding sounds like a very stoical attitude; the usual completion of the phrase is 'of a bad job'. Paul is determined that he is not going to give in to that pressure: 'It seemed to him that to sacrifice himself in a marriage he did not want would be degrading, and would undo all his life, make it a nullity' (322). The word 'sacrifice' proves to be thematic, though here it seems literal. When Paul is having his affair with Clara he is consciously going against the code, though paradoxically his mother feels he is safe with a married woman. He talks bluntly both to his mother and to Miriam. His mother says '... you know what folk are, and if once she gets talked about —' and he replies 'Then she must pay, we both must pay. Folk are so frightened of paying' (358–9). Miriam makes the point that under the double standard the woman pays more: 'The man does as he likes —' When he replies, 'Then let the woman also', she says, 'You don't understand what a woman forfeits —' He counters '... if a woman's got nothing but her fair fame to feed on — why, it's thin tack, and a donkey would die of it' (361). This is brave talk, but is all taken at the level of what Lawrence called idea and will: what one thinks. It is not so easy when one is dealing at the deeper level of what one mysteriously is.

It is becoming clear that another answer to the question 'What is the novel about?' is, love and marriage at the turn of the century, when the fierce traditional morality was first being questioned. What the old tribal rules controlled was sexuality: if young people got caught, they had to marry. If they married, they had to stay married, like it or not. This background of rule-governed behaviour is in the first half of the novel very guarded about sexuality, as one of the things that is not discussed, not even mentioned: hence the coded messages from William and Sue. In the second Part,

Paul has sexual experiences which are actually described, and it is difficult for the reader born after 1945 to grasp how upsetting this was in 1913. Not only that: Lawrence also conveys that sexual acts, which still to many writers seem mechanical and repetitive, are actually different in their meanings, according to the feeling they express.

Paul's experience with Miriam is in the first place willed, by him. He has told her that he thinks it ought now to be the next thing they do, he is of an age, and they both think, don't they, that it ought to be a wonderful thing. He ignores for the moment, and she suppresses, the inborn virginity which is the shared consequence of their parentage, and she enters into it in a spirit of conscious self-sacrifice. What he feels afterwards is a revulsion – a sense of deathliness – which he cannot understand.

When he turns to Clara he is more free of his psychic burden simply because he does not have the affinity with her which he has with Miriam (she is not so like his mother). The sexuality is liberating. The great scene downstairs in Clara's house after her mother has gone up to bed is by a long way the most explicit in English literature up to this point, especially now that Garnett's small but crucial cuts are restored: for instance, the curious little observation that in Clara's bedroom Paul sees a pair of her stockings, on an impulse puts them on, and knows that he must have her. In 1913, this seemed obscene; now, it combines insight with neat symbolism. I say 'explicit', but might have said 'poetic', for the imagery of the cut passages suggests a literary debt, to Baudelaire. The other great scene of love-making, outdoors in the field with the peewits screaming, also has a literary cast: it is as if Lawrence is trying to imagine what this great experience might be like, and succeeding pretty well. The failure with Miriam, on the other hand, is painfully real.

Paul Morel's problems are symptomatic of the difficulties many people face in arriving at a good relationship. Perhaps they always have, but now there is a greater consciousness of their nature. And that is another part of the theme: the 'dynastic' nature of the novel, the fact that it follows two generations, implies that a social, almost a tribal unselfconsciousness in an older generation has to be followed by a personal self-consciousness in the next one if the problems are to be understood, even more if they are to be overcome. This raises the question, do you overcome things by understanding them (the premiss of psychoanalysis)?

The merely tribal marriage which is the background and a recurrent observed event is evidently rejected at a conscious level by Paul; and he presses this advanced or liberated view on his mother, who listens as a sceptical former participant now an observer, or on Miriam and Clara, who both have feminist leanings which give them another perspective. What he also presses on them is a need for a love which is frank about sexual need, and acts out that frankness. He talks Miriam, against her deeper inclination, into a sexual relationship, and is then dismayed to find how much he is himself unsatisfied by her sacrifice. With Clara he feels it is more 'impersonal'; but it is still his demand on her, and at the end she too rejects him for wanting it rather than her. What he does not know is the extent to which his demand on them is denatured by his own psychic deformation. All his ideas are only that, ideas: good in themselves as counters in a discussion, but not actually the deep springs of his actions.

A marriage which was not tribally enforced, seems to have been a love-match, can still turn out wrong. The great example is the marriage of Gertrude Coppard and Walter Morel, which begins with the glamorous night of a Christmas dance and becomes a lifelong conflict. This is the central structural element of the novel in the sense that it determines both the duple pattern, of the two sons, their fates worked out in the two Parts, and the triple pattern of Paul's relationships with his three women. The parental conflict dominates Part I: it has counterparts in Part II in the marriages of Miriam's parents, the Leiverses, and of Clara and Baxter Dawes. The events themselves are the main thread of Part I; in Part II Paul's blind actions are a consequence and a comment; we sense him groping towards, but never quite reaching, a conscious view of the effect on him of his parents' relationship.

We have seen that when he talks to Miriam about the sense he has made of William's death, he cannot go on to see that the parents' failure and the mother's dominance are factors. He comes to this very slowly, perhaps never perceives it squarely, perhaps cannot afford to. It is, rather, refracted by other elements of his experience, and primarily by the marriage of Baxter and Clara Dawes, which is seen, but slowly, to follow the pattern of the Morels.

The episode with Clara, being mostly Lawrence's imagining, is written off by many readers as less important than his other experiences, which are 'real'. In the terms of Lawrence's letter to Garnett, here is the other son 'going for passion'; it makes sense as the next move in his story, but feels a bit made-up. Here too the common instinct is basically right; the episode is not convincing in the same painful way as the rest of the book. Nonetheless Lawrence uses it very subtly in so far as he shows it to be on the surface a form of un-conscious escape for Paul, or a false way out of his problem; while below the surface it gives him a parable or model which takes him closer, almost all the way, to a true picture of his parents.

Here the duple rhythm operates. Certain judgements in Part I are qualified in Part II. Think for instance of the categorical statements where the narrative simply gives Mrs Morel's point of view, and then issues in statements such as: 'At last Mrs Morel despised her husband' (22); 'she destroyed him' (25). A little more even-handedly, it also points out that 'She could not be content with the little he might be' (25). As for him, feeling himself displaced by the children, 'he half acquiesced' (62). So far as he is given an inner life at all, it is a sad one: 'His soul would reach out in its blind way to her, and find her gone. He felt a sort of emptiness, almost like a vacuum in his soul' (63). (The notation quietly planted but not developed there, the sense of emptiness, a void, is crucially developed later.)

Paul's first attempt really to reflect on the Morels' marriage is triggered by trying to make sense of that of the Daweses. As he talks to Clara about it, trying to understand what happened, an opinion crystallises, and surprisingly, it is hostile to her. She explains that she had thought she loved Dawes, and 'he wanted me'. 'Sort of walked into it without thinking?' Paul asks. The marriage went wrong, she says, because Dawes never waked her, 'never got there'. She re-defines this mysterious formula as 'He wanted to bully me, because he hadn't got me. And then I felt as if I wanted to run ... he seemed as if he couldn't get *at* me, really. And then he got brutal.' Paul pursues her: did she ever give Dawes a chance 'to come near to you ... I suppose he couldn't *make* himself mean everything to you?' (317–18). They feel they are out of their depth, and the conversation lapses. Later, he renews the attack (for so it has become): 'Were you horrid with Baxter Dawes? ... weren't you horrid with him? Didn't you do something that knocked him to pieces? ... I feel you did something to him – sort of broke him – broke his manliness ... I believe you did him as much damage, more than he did you, by sort of cutting him underneath, and making him feel ashamed ... Making him feel as if he were nothing – *I* know' (319–20; cut). It is as if he is speaking for his father, without realising it. If *he* now knows, it is because his own family background provides the parallel case, and he can speak out of it instinctively without reflecting on what he is saying.

In a later conversation with Miriam, it is she who makes the comparison. Developing the 'sleeping beauty' fairy-tale analogy, Paul says 'With him, she [Clara] was only half alive, the rest was dormant ... And she *had* to be awakened.' That seems to justify his own role, as useful prince. It is Miriam who says 'It was something like your mother and father.' He half agrees, but fends off total identification by making the remarkable distinction that his mother 'got *real* joy and satisfaction out of my father at first. I believe she had a passion for him ... That's what one *must have* ... the real, real flame of feeling through another person ... See, my mother looks as if she'd *had* everything that was necessary for her living and developing ... she had the real thing. She knows − she has been there' (361−2). 'There' is Clara's word, and its recurrences in the novel give it a strange force, to do with really existing, being oneself, and being oneself for another person. He may be implying: that's what I'm now doing for Clara; but, for the moment he is speaking for his mother. He knows that; but not what he is implying about his father, still less that he is making it possible for a listener to reflect that his failure with Clara is exactly described by her own earlier words about Dawes.

There is also something romantic and limited about this description of the Morels; it leaves out of account their struggle, the deadlock, and especially how any blame for it might be apportioned. If the accusation levelled at Clara, that it was more her fault, and she had been 'horrid' to Dawes, strikes the reader as a deflected criticism of his mother for her part in all that, a not unjust one, it is crucial that he does not see it.

One might indulge the paradox that the Paul who can reach this point of near-detachment and near-insight could, if he were a writer, *almost* go on to write a book like *Sons and Lovers*. To do so he would indeed have to imagine something like this whole strand of the novel, the part which is 'not real' precisely because it goes beyond his own experience; and this in order to reach a point of true detachment, of self-knowledge and self-criticism by showing the hidden pattern in his own behaviour. And Lawrence himself *has* done that: the episode with Clara shows it. We can see that Paul's 'going for passion' is only half the point. He could get passion anywhere: enlightenment is quite another thing. He does not quite get it; it is in the nature of the case that he can't; but we do, and it is the author who gives it to us in this profoundly indirect way.

The formal symmetries start to do this for us, especially the duple one: not as mere pattern, but as significance. In Part I it has been very carefully established that the two sons, first William, and then Paul, are jealous of their father, are his rivals, resent the father's bond with the mother; both of them respond to his provocations with an approach to violence.

Paul nearly fights his father because he interrupts what is to all intents a love-scene with the mother. As a child Paul even wishes his father dead, prays that he may be killed 'at pit' (85). Now in Part II he is in love with a strong-minded married woman with a defeated husband; he feels a conscious rivalry with the other man. Dawes is a working man, like Morel: manly, unselfconscious, falling into drunkenness because undermined by the failure of the marriage. He and Paul frankly hate each other, and yet the jealousy is a mysterious bond between them. There is a murderous fight; Paul nearly throttles Dawes, who gives Paul a brutal kicking and leaves him for dead. But Paul makes contact with him later, is reconciled and as it were formally returns his wife to him: she is really his, in a way that he can never allow that his mother is his father's, and should be returned to *him*.

Because of his partial vision, Paul is startled when at the end of their affair Clara accuses him of just the inadequacies she had found in Dawes, and in just the same mysterious terms: she says to him, as if Gipsy had suddenly been given a consciousness and had turned on William, it is as if 'you only loved me at night'. 'The night is free to you', he replies (403), but she won't be fobbed off with a split-off part of him: 'You've never come near to me. You can't come out of yourself, you can't' (406–7). With Miriam too he thinks he is ending their affair as a matter of conscious choice, and is taken aback when he is accused of being himself an unsatisfactory partner in the relationship: irritated, she says he is like a child of four, producing the telling response: 'All right, if I'm a child of four, what do you want me for. *I* don't want another mother' (340). There is the problem; in important ways Miriam is like his mother, which is why there is an inner resistance in him, which she divines: '"It has been one long battle between us – you fighting away from me ... It has always been you fighting me off." ... He sat aghast ... Then it had been monstrous' (341). The word is his.

At last, at the conscious level, he attempts to grasp these failures. There is a touching moment when he says to his mother: 'You know mother, I think there must be something the matter with me, that I *can't* love ... I feel sometimes as if I wronged my women, mother ... to *give* myself to them in marriage − I couldn't. I couldn't belong to them.' She says he hasn't met the right woman. He says, and he may now really know the truth of it, 'And I never shall meet the right woman while you live.' As for her reaction, Lawrence only says:

His mother turned away her face, sat looking across the room, very quiet, grave, with something of renunciation ...

Now she began to feel again tired, as if she were done. (395)

The implications delicately hinted at in 'grave', 'renunciation' and 'done' are silently fulfilled in the plot; she begins to die, as if something in her knows she must.

Other connections begin to be made in the mind. At a merely verbal level, the fight with Dawes may remind the reader who knows Lawrence's own reading, of Scott's 'Lady of the Lake' and George Eliot's *Romola* (Lawrence was fascinated by the idea of one man strangling another). But where is it that Paul and Dawes meet and fight at night? Not perhaps at a place where three roads cross, where Oedipus, unknowing, killed his father? No; actually outside Nottingham, between one stile and the next. Nonetheless, the scene is carefully set, in the quasi-mythopoeic terms which the novel deploys, analysed in the next section of this study:

The town ceases almost abruptly on the edge of a steep hollow. There the houses with their yellow lights stand up against the darkness. He went over the stile and dropped quickly into the hollow of the fields ... Behind, the houses stood on the brim of the dip, black against the sky, like wild beasts glaring curiously with yellow eyes down into the darkness. It was the town that seemed savage and uncouth, glaring on the clouds at the back of him. (409)

In the Dawes affair Lawrence *is* very subtly rewriting the Oedipus legend. The novel has Paul fall in love with women in whom we can see something of his mother, and he half-wants to kill, but importantly is reconciled with, a man in whom he can almost see his father. It is a kind of deflection:

he can sympathise with Dawes, instead of his actual father; and the relationship with Clara has no point when his mother is dead. That with his mother is severed, but not resolved, by her death, which is the equivalent of Jocasta's suicide. He can return Clara to her husband as a sad substitute for returning his mother to his father.

Once one has seen one such link, other memories stir: what was Hamlet's mother called? Gertrude, like Mrs Morel. So that when Paul says, just after he has nearly fought his father: 'Sleep with Annie, mother, not with him ... Don't sleep with him, mother' (254), we are surely meant to think of Hamlet saying, just after he has killed Polonius, thinking it was the hated uncle who has usurped his own as well as his father's love for his mother:

> Goodnight – but go not to my uncle's bed:
> Assume a virtue if you have it not.

We know too that Lawrence saw Ibsen's *Ghosts* in Munich in the summer of 1912. (By an extraordinary coincidence, he saw both *Ghosts* and *Hamlet* in rapid succession in Gargnano in December 1912 and January 1913, and this triggered a whole theme in *Twilight in Italy*.) But he knew Ibsen well; *Hedda Gabler* gives him his reveller with leaves and berries in her hair. In *Ghosts* the son Oswald is also a painter, we remember; and the mother looks back on a bad marriage to a drunk, but comes to feel that what had really animated him as a young man was 'the joy of living' which she has repressed in him. The son's heredity manifests itself as syphilis: he knows that this will degenerate into dementia, and hopes for a moment that the girl he discovers to be his bastard half-sister will have the strength to give him the fatal dose of morphia he has acquired for the time when it is needed; but now the mother must do this for him in his total dependence: strong curtain. Lawrence inverts this situation and takes the melodrama out of it. His painter and the sister give the morphia to the dying mother. It is possible that Lawrence really did this; but I think it is imagined, and that it is Lawrence's subtle reversal of Ibsen's situation. The duple rhythm is seen here too.

William dies of erysipelas, Gertrude Morel of cancer. Those are the real immediate medical conditions, like Oswald's syphilis in *Ghosts*. Paul is able to divine the symbolism, the deeper life-threat, in the case of William, but not for his mother (Lawrence does this explicitly in the letter to Garnett). And of course Paul cannot diagnose his own trouble, though he becomes aware that he has one.

The old Greek myth puts things in stark and absolute terms: the son does kill his father, marries the mother, has children by her and must be punished by self-mutilation and exile if the curse on the city-state is to be removed. Freud's psychoanalytical appropriation of the myth is a little less stark; the son does want to kill the father and marry the mother, but this is metaphorised into a fantasy indulged by the infant. Ibsen's metaphorisation turns the hereditary effect of marital conflict into a positivist upshot, syphilis, and makes the son literally dependent on the mother for life-support and euthanasia. Lawrence on the other hand sees the heredity, the result of conflict in the previous generation, as what we daily see it to be. The son's attempt to place his love elsewhere than in the mother and his rivalry other than in his father is frustrated; he is as if condemned to repeat their mistakes, in subtly disguised forms: finds that the other women he tries to love embody aspects of his mother, which is both why he chooses them and why in the end he rejects them; what is more, the loved women find aspects of his parents, including his father, in him: his heredity is his failure to be 'there', to come out of himself.

So the repetitions in the plot are not merely formal: they convey what Lawrence in the letter to Garnett called his 'theme': it is a specifically modern tragic principle. The classic dynastic curse is replaced by the psychological truth that family relationships, without which we do not become persons with identities, also inflict damage, which we may see repeated in generation after generation. It is in the nature of the case that the protagonists are both agents and victims: above all that they do not have full consciousness of what they are and do. The answer to critics who say that the narrator is too identified with Paul's point of view must be that to have that voice acting as analyst as we go along would undermine the essential principle that these things are difficult, for most people impossible, to discover. Half the problem is the unconsciousness of it. To have an unconscious protagonist is, in Henry James's terms, correctly to dramatise. It is for the reader to discover, with the necessary degree of difficulty, what the characters cannot see, and the way to do this is to follow the implications of the careful structure, shaped with an art which Lawrence is not usually credited with.

Chapter 3

Form: imagery as structure

So the novel is also about degrees of consciousness, with a range from total unselfconsciousness in Morel, to a consciousness which directs a dominating and unself-critical will in Mrs Morel, to a self-consciousness in Paul and Miriam which is extreme but not self-directing. There is an implication about the two generations. Morel is tribal, archaic, almost mythical: it might have been wonderful to have been him in some earlier time. Mrs Morel is of the nineteenth century: genuinely pious and moral, aware of the cost to herself of being so, but not of the cost to others. Paul and Miriam are of this century at its beginning: highly conscious, uncertainly feeling their way into the future. Miriam carries much more of the past with her: Paul loves her because she is in important ways like his mother, and this is why he must also reject her, so that she becomes his sacrificial victim.

Lawrence needs to dramatise these consciousnesses and give us the ways in which they instinctively apprehend their world. This is not so much a theme, more like the continuous but variegated medium in which everything is realised; the way in which the centres of consciousness are aware of their world, make sense of it − and project their own inner world. The only adequate language is metaphor; an analytical prose transcription would present an objective world, uniform, clear, rationalised, where once more the narrative voice tells us what to think and how to feel, by arbitrating between viewpoints.

An advantage of metaphor is that shared or related or contrasted imagery can indicate overarching similarities of feeling (as between Mrs Morel and Miriam, for instance) or sharp distinctions of personality. So metaphors too can be structural. The challenge, as with the narrative voice, is to perform the arbitration: whose consciousness is this? Is it a dramatisation by the author, a projection by the character, is it universal, is it idiosyncratically Lawrence's? I contend that, here too, in offering a felt world which is originally personal and departs from a child's vision, he is offering to be representative, indeed universal. I enter it with what I take to be one of the main components of the metaphorical structure. It could not be more simple.

There was no electricity in poor homes at this time, often no gas. The child at night could ponder the difference between four kinds of light; indoors there was candle-light with its soft lapping flame, or the oil-lamp burning more intensely, often smokily. There might be gas-light, which burned rather like the portable spirit-lamp; this by pump action compressed air and fuel into gas, which escaped through a delicate lacy mantle to burn as incandescence, making a hissing noise and a hard white light unlike the soft golden light of candle and oil. Outside, the street gas-lamps used the same mantle device to cast a circle of light around the tall lamppost. In all cases the circle implied safety within it. If you had your back to the light you had safety behind you, and looked outward to a darkness, night, which might feel a threat; it depended how you felt about what was behind you and what you 'fronted', to use Lawrence's word. This homely metaphor is at the root of a great ramifying image-cluster. The basic contrast is between what is within the circle: warm, safe, solid, stable, and what is outside: dark, empty, endless, threatening. Another contrast sets white light against gold. Both can be identified with feelings about people. There is a strong sense also of what is inside a boundary, safe; or outside, and dangerous. So one feeling mutates into another as one image calls up another.

Mrs Morel in the opening pages of the book is seen waiting for her husband to come home: the first instance of the behaviour-pattern. The light has faded, the twilight sunk. She is alone, but used to it. The children are upstairs asleep, 'so, it seemed, her home was there behind her, fixed and stable' (13). There is no overt figure in the language, but the words 'behind', 'fixed', 'stable' acquire great force; are examples of Lawrence's way of transmitting a poetic charge through the prosaic-seeming conductors which link associative fields or even call up inversions. Already, the words imply something about her as well as her world. The figures themselves begin to appear a few pages later, and are used to give a perception of the young miner Walter Morel such that the whole of the rest of the book cannot destroy this first impression; it is one of the pillars on which it is built. He is a positive, if a lost one; an ideal.

It starts as description. Morel was '... then twenty-seven years old [Lawrence's age in 1912–13]. He was well-set-up, erect and very smart. He had wavy, black hair ...' There follows an adjective which one learns to recognise as Lawrence's approval-indicator: 'His cheeks were ruddy, and his red, moist mouth was noticeable because he laughed so often and so heartily.' 'She herself was opposite', we are told, '... loved ideas, and was considered very intellectual' (17). The metaphors begin to emerge. 'He danced well, as if it were natural and joyous in him to dance' (William inherits this); he has 'a certain subtle exultation like glamour in his movement, and his face the flower of his body, ruddy, with tumbled black hair, and laughing alike whatever partner he bowed above' (18). Flowers are an important part of the image-tissue; but the clinching image comes on the same page:

Therefore the dusky, golden softness of this man's sensuous flame of life, that flowed from off his flesh like the flame from a candle, not baffled and gripped into incandescence by thought and spirit as her life was, seemed to her something wonderful, beyond her. (18)

The candle-flame is contrasted with the pressure-lamp; the one associated with warmth and naturalness, the other with thought and spirit; 'baffled and gripped' implies conflict and frustration. It is the distinction between happy unselfconsciousness rooted in its own life and the consciousness which separates from life. 'Something wonderful, beyond her' is a religious feeling.

The reader familiar with Lawrence's letters immediately makes a connection with the letter to Collings written not long after he had finished the novel, on 17 January 1913:

My great religion is a belief in the blood, the flesh, as being wiser than the intellect. We can go wrong in our minds. But what our blood feels and believes and says, is always true. The intellect is only a bit and a bridle. What do I care about knowledge. All I want is to answer to my blood, direct, without fribbling intervention of mind, or moral, or what not. I conceive a man's body as a kind of flame, like a candle flame forever upright and yet flowing: and the intellect is just the light that is shed onto the things around. And I am not so much concerned with the things around; – which is really mind: – but with the mystery of the flame forever flowing, coming God knows how from out of practically nowhere, and being *itself*, whatever there is around it, that it lights up. We have got so ridiculously mindful, that we never know that we ourselves are anything – we think there are only the objects we shine upon. And there the poor flame goes on burning ignored, to produce this light. And instead of chasing the mystery in the fugitive, half lighted things outside us, we ought to look at ourselves and say 'My God, I am myself!' That is why I like to live in Italy. The people are so unconscious. They only feel and want: they don't know. We know too much. No, we only *think* we know such a lot. A flame isn't a flame because it lights up two, or twenty objects on a table. It's a flame because it is itself. And we have forgotten ourselves. We are Hamlet without the Prince of Denmark. We cannot *be*. 'To be or not to be' – it is the question with us now, by Jove. And nearly every Englishman says 'Not to be.' So he goes in for Humanitarianism and such like forms of not-being. The real way of living is to answer to one's wants. Not 'I want to light up with my intelligence as many things as possible' – but 'For the living of my full flame – I want that liberty, I want that woman, I want that pound of peaches, I want to go to sleep, I want to go to the pub and have a good time, I want to look a beastly swell today, I want to kiss that girl, I want to insult that man.' – Instead of that, all these wants, which are there whether-or-not, are utterly ignored, and we talk about some sort of ideas. (I, 503–4)

So Walter Morel, if only for a moment in the courtship, if only as representative of an ideal that has been lost in him or in his generation, is identified with the positives in the letter, and the emblem of the candle-flame and its golden light. It is opposed in the novel by the fierce white light of incandescence, which is associated with mind, consciousness. Mind itself, in the letter, is the source of what is wrong with us, yet it will not escape the reader that Lawrence has only the mind to appeal to if we are, necessary paradox, to be aware of our plight. But he is in the letter as in the novel using the language which resolves the paradox: metaphor, which is feeling as thinking. Mrs Morel's superiority might seem real to many people because it resides in this intelligence, associated with a strong will; yet the novel conveys how much this is a burden – not just for her – and the source of conflict. Here again are the pregnant words in which Lawrence implies what the conflict does to Morel: this plants another term in the image system, to be unfolded with the action:

His soul would reach out in its blind way to her, and find her gone. He felt a sort of emptiness, almost like a vacuum in his soul. (63)

Against her sense of being 'fixed and stable' in her moral certainties, her intelligence, her sense of duty, her light thrown on the things around her, his light has gone out, he is blind and unsupported internally; what in her is pumped-up moral pressure is in him drawn out, collapsing.

This complex sense, where the images and insights are beginning to extend or complement each other, is amplified in the great scene at the end of the first chapter, the first of the mysterious night-scenes, where the reader, conscious of the 'poetry', may struggle for a meaning. The Morels have a long, fierce and realistic quarrel (abridged by Garnett) when he comes home drunk. She says, 'Do you think it's for *you* I stop – do you think I'd stop one minute for *you* –' and he retorts 'Go then ... Go!' She replies no, 'I've got those children to see to.' She uses them against him. He 'thrust her forth', drops into his chair, and falls asleep (33).

As psychological realism, what follows is profoundly imagined as the process of her coming back from a state of being beyond herself as well as literally outside the house, to a state of conscious self-possession again, and return to the home. The things she notices outside are there with a super-real otherness. Is that, one asks, a way of representing her consciousness? What is outside, what she is thrust into, is 'a great, white light, that fell cold on her'. It is 'an immense gulf of white light, the moon streaming high in face of her, the moonlight standing up from the hills in front, and filling the valley ..., almost blindingly' (34). As consciousness begins to return:

> She became aware of something about her. With an effort, she roused herself, to see what it was that penetrated her consciousness. The tall white lilies were reeling in the moonlight, and the air was charged with their perfume, as with a presence. Mrs Morel gasped slightly in fear. She touched the big, pallid flowers on their petals, then shivered. They seemed to be stretching in the moonlight. She put her hand into one white bin: the gold scarcely showed on her fingers by moonlight. She bent down, to look at the bin-ful of yellow pollen: but it only appeared dusky. Then she drank a deep draught of the scent. It almost made her dizzy. (33–4)

The gold which appears 'dusky' because cancelled by the moonlight reminds us of the same word used about Morel's glamour: the 'dusky, golden softness' of the candle-flame. The pollen may remind us that she is carrying Paul, and the lilies are the emblems of the Annunciation; so is she carrying a sort of saviour, or are we being told that though this is her third child she is still essentially a virgin, like Mrs Leivers later after her seven children (323)? When she looks through the window to attract Morel's attention 'the lamp was burning smokily', which suggests something about him; when she manages to get him to let her in again 'there stood the silver grey night, fearful to him, after the tawny light of the lamp'. As she goes to bed 'she smiled faintly to see her face all smeared with the yellow dust of lilies. She brushed it off' (35–6). Is that a suggestion of something in him that she has also brushed off?

Mrs Morel herself warns us not to rush into easy algebraic substitutions. To the young minister Mr Heaton, who wants to make the miracle at Cana represent a sacred transubstantiation of the 'blood' of all partners in marriage she says 'No ... don't make things into symbols. Say: "It was a wedding, and the wine ran out"' (45; cut). She points out that wine is not beer – not so intoxicating, she thinks; so in helping out in a family embarrassment Jesus was not creating a social problem. But then, she would say that; Heaton's interpretation is not one she wants to hear; the little piece of characterisation leaves the question of interpretation open, except as a warning not to be too quick to find a meaning. For she has provided an interpretation too, very much her own, and reductive.

One might suggest that neither Morel nor Mrs Morel are night-people; what they contest is the lighted home interior, that security. When he thrusts her out, it is into a real night out there; but its extraordinary white light, which contrasts at the end with the tawny light of the lamp inside, partly conveys the opposition between him and her, partly universalises it. The conflict, as the letter to Collings suggests, is between the instinctive nature of the man and the mental nature of the woman. The moonlight falling on things outside lights them up in exactly the way the letter speaks of the mind, and it is cold and alienating.

A few pages later we find another extraordinary scene: one of the passages one would use to demonstrate the power of Lawrence's writing. Things are seen with visionary clarity; and again there is a charge of mystery which hints at meanings. We are given the other term of the sun/moon polarity:

> She went over the sheep-bridge and across a corner of the meadow to the cricket ground. The meadows seemed one space of ripe, evening light, whispering with the distant mill-race. She sat on a seat under the alders in the cricket ground, and fronted the evening. Before her, level and solid, spread the big green cricket-field, like the bed of a sea of light. Children played in the bluish shadow of the pavilion. Many rooks, high up, came cawing home across the softly woven sky. They stooped in a long curve down into the golden glow, concentrating, cawing, wheeling like black flakes on a slow vortex, over a tree-clump that made a dark boss among the pasture. (49)

This is beautiful, certainly, but the notations spread beyond the context. That she 'fronted' the evening seems characteristic of Mrs Morel's will and consciousness, her courage. The 'sea of light' and the 'golden glow' also begin to seem like motifs, since white and gold light are beginning to operate like heraldic alternatives. It is important that she has an element of the golden glow in her. The word 'space' (what one fronts; what seems an emptiness, a void, a vacuum) comes to bear a great weight of meaning. It recurs in the continuation:

... already the under-shadows were smouldering. Away at the grange, one side of the hay-stacks was lit up, the other sides blue-grey. A wagon of sheaves rocked small across the melting yellow light.

The sun was going down. Every open evening, the hills of Derbyshire were blazed over with red sunset. Mrs Morel watched the sun sink from the glistening sky, leaving a soft flower-blue overhead, while the western space went red, as if all the fire had swum down there, leaving the bell cast flawless blue. The mountain-ash berries across the field stood fierily out from the dark leaves, for a moment. A few shocks of corn in a corner of the fallow stood up as if alive: she imagined them bowing: perhaps her son would be a Joseph. In the east, a mirrored sunset floated pink opposite the west's scarlet. The big haystacks on the hill-side that butted into the glare, went cold. (49–50)

It goes on being beautiful, but is not mere fine writing – a descriptive set-piece; this is the vision that the woman, with her baby on her knee, intensely sees, and one detail is projected into a homage to the child. The sudden thought that it may be a remarkable man, combined with the outside glory, transforms her mood again. Now it is the sun which is bringing her insights, not the moon. 'She had dreaded this baby like a catastrophe, because of her feeling for her husband.' She has a moment of guilt for not having wanted it, which transforms into a wave of love. This mood-change, a psychic process as precisely notated as the external scene, produces a strange action:

Once more she was aware of the sun lying red on the rim of the hill opposite. She suddenly held up the child in her hands.

'Look!' she said. 'Look, my pretty!'

She thrust the infant forward to the crimson, throbbing sun, almost with relief. She saw him lift his little fist. Then she put him to her bosom again, ashamed almost of her impulse to give him back again whence he came. (51)

These are instinctive religious gestures. The holding up of the child is part-sacrifice, part-dedication; the child's gesture is part-defiance, part-greeting, as if to an ultimate father.

She decides at that moment to call him Paul, a name associated with dramatic conversion. The novel is full of Christian echoes, as well as pointing out into the cosmos in a way that is not specifically Christian. Pondered, this can be seen as a way of removing the other-worldliness from religious feeling, of naturalising it into the everyday. The 'Foreword' takes up and formalises this disseminated set of hints. The young Paul, when he reaches the age of religious consciousness puts his sense of the divinity at the heart of things in a neat formulation: 'It's not religious to be religious ... a crow is religious when it sails across the sky. But it only does it because it feels itself carried to where it's going ... God doesn't *know* things, he *is* things − ' (291).

Paul's friends jokingly call him 'Postle. The sense that he is a dedicated spirit, and that this is conveyed on the authority of the sun itself − that he is therefore somehow 'of' that realm of golden light − this vision is given to Miriam too. She divines it, that seems to be the word, and it makes her something of a priestess, like the mother:

He remained concentrated in the middle of the road. Beyond, one rift of rich gold in that colourless grey evening seemed to make him stand out in dark relief. She saw him slender and firm, as if the setting sun had given him to her ... Quivering as at some 'Annunciation', she went slowly forward. (201)

That Miriam and Mrs Morel have the same vision strengthens the affinity between them. Mrs Morel's life-flame had been described as 'baffled and gripped into incandescence by thought and spirit'. Is the word 'spirit' the source of the spirit-lamp image, or generated by it? Both. The image has also secured the association of the word 'gripped', so that one calls up the other. Of Miriam it is said, in a startling light-image:

All the light of Miriam's body was in her eyes, which were usually dark as a dark church, but could flame with light like a conflagration ... She might have been one of the women who went with Mary when Jesus was dead. (184)

This is amplified in a way that sends us back to the spirit-lamp source: 'Everything was gripped stiff with intensity, and her effort, over-charged, closed in on itself.' The covert link is

renewed a few pages later, in the scene where Paul is irritated
with her even as he is teaching her: '... things came slowly
to her. And when she held herself in a grip, seemed so utterly
humble before the lesson, it made his blood rouse' (188).

The image crystallises a few pages later, when the affinity
between Miriam and Mrs Morel is touched on. The remarkable
thing is that when they are juxtaposed the tonality of coldness
and white light is concentrated entirely in Miriam, while Mrs
Morel retains her part in the sun-realm of warmth. Is this
what Jessie felt to be Lawrence's unconscious bias?

> He loved to sit at home, alone with his mother at night, working and
> working ... looking up ... he would rest his eyes for a moment on her
> face, that was bright with living warmth, and he returned gladly to
> his work.
> 'I can do my best things when you sit there ... mother,' he said ...
> ... And he, with all his soul's intensity directing his pencil, could
> feel her warmth inside him like strength ...
> He was conscious only when stimulated. A sketch finished, he
> always wanted to take it to Miriam. Then he was stimulated into
> knowledge of the work he had produced unconsciously. In contact
> with Miriam, he gained insight, his vision went deeper. From his
> mother he drew the life warmth, the strength to produce; Miriam
> urged this warmth into intensity like a white light. (190)

(And yet, in a passage cut by Garnett, the long episode where he
waits for Miriam in the lending library on Thursday night, there
is one of Lawrence's strangest notations: 'But she would come.
It still felt warm and rich, just in front, and night went no further
than the moment when she would arrive' (191). 'Just in front',
one learns, is where space starts: at the mouth, at the breast.)

A few pages later there follows the scene of the wild rose-bush
at night: another of the powerful moments when the reader
reaches for some descriptive term, and falls back on 'poetic'.
It shows that what Miriam does for Paul, he also does for her,
but with a quite distinct personal effect: 'Till he had seen it,
she felt it had not come into her soul. Only he could make it
her own, immortal' (195). It is another mysterious scene, of
otherness, of white light in the darkness around, of coming
into consciousness of the other, of appropriating it or releasing
it into power:

The tree was tall and straggling. It had thrown its briars over a hawthorn bush, and its long streamers trailed thick, right down to the grass, splashing the darkness everywhere with great spilt stars, pure white. In bosses of ivory and in large splashed stars the roses gleamed on the darkness of foliage and stems and grass. Paul and Miriam stood close together, silent, and watched. Point after point, the steady roses shone out to them, seeming to kindle something in their souls. The dusk came like smoke around, and still did not put out the roses. (195)

And the light shineth in darkness, and the darkness comprehended it not, one remembers, from John's Gospel. It is like an Annunciation again: 'She was pale and expectant with wonder, her lips were parted, and her dark eyes lay open to him. His look seemed to travel down into her. Her soul quivered. It was the communion she wanted' (195–6). He completes, or defuses, the situation by producing a metaphor for her (the roses are like butterflies) and the tension is discharged: we are left with the sense that this, for them, and especially for her, is a spiritual substitute for sexuality.

Miriam performs an essential role for Paul as artist: 'She brought forth to him his imaginations' (241). He needs her to give him consciousness of what he has produced in his spontaneities, and she needs to do this for him. At more than one point Paul rebels against being used this way, feels she only wants him for what she can 'get out' of him ('I'm so damned spiritual with *you* always', 226). His revulsion from this role, in which one essential part of him is deeply complicit, chimes with what Mrs Morel feels about Miriam: 'She wants to absorb him ... draw him out and absorb him till there is nothing left of him, even for himself ... she will suck him up' (230). Paul puts this woundingly to her, turning his need and his own related nature into a charge against her: 'You don't want to love – your eternal and abnormal craving is to be loved. You aren't positive, you're negative. You absorb, absorb, as if you must fill yourself up with love, because you've got a shortage somewhere' (258). The deeper sense of that, the hidden metaphor, reminds us of that vacuum which has been waiting for the link. Just after Mrs Morel used the words 'suck him up', we read 'there was a great hollow of darkness fronting him'. So the vacuum is projected outside, onto the world, the night. It is a sharp intensification of Morel's dim sense of hollowness. But it contrasts with a counterpoising certainty in Paul, what he feels behind him, that Morel cannot have:

He had come back to his mother. Hers was the strongest tie in his life. When he thought round, Miriam shrank away. There was a vague, unreal feel about her. And nobody else mattered. There was one place in the world that stood solid and did not melt into unreality: the place where his mother was. Everybody else could grow shadowy, almost non-existent to him, but she could not. It was as if the pivot and pole of his life, from which he could not escape, was his mother. (261)

It seems prosaic. But one thinks back to Mrs Morel, 'fixed and stable' in her home in the very first pages; now she inhabits the one place that will not 'melt into unreality'. The hint of metaphor in 'pivot and pole' gives the sense of a something revolving, a circle, perhaps of light; within the circle is an upright figure.

There is a persistent theme of taking an experience to another and having it validated – and so of being dependent on that person for the support. It begins as a series of simple observations. 'All his [William's] pride was built on *her* seeing him' (76; cut). 'No one told him [Morel] anything ... Nothing had really taken place in them, until it was told to their mother' (87). This is a natural process, in itself; it strengthens Mrs Morel's identity as it undercuts Morel's. It grows into a kind of psychic cancer. Mrs Morel becomes jealous of Miriam for receiving what she herself once received, perceives Miriam's need as a ravening demand. Paul is perplexed at discovering this need in Miriam, even though it answers to his own need to have a kindred spirit to confirm his creativity. He too 'felt that she wanted the soul out of his body, and not him ... wanted to draw all of him into her' (231–2). It goes so far as to make him feel 'You switch me off somewhere, and project me out of myself'. He has 'A sort of disseminated consciousness ... as if my body were lying empty, as if I were in the other things – clouds and water' (232). This remarkable perception of a psychic state also asks to be linked backward to Morel's 'vacuum', and forward to the final paragraphs of the whole book, where that sense of vacuum, suction, permeability, outward drift to death is given its culminating force as life-threat.

The power of the whole set of notations is that it progresses from ordinary childish openness, trust and dependence into pathological forms in the adult, and shows that no character is uninvolved. The positive forces — stability, solidity, support, warmth, love — are located in the mother through the analogues (lamplight in the home, and the lamppost outside). The universal night, the darkness, the space, which 'scoop' at the land (101; see also 267, 313, 354) and into which he fears to be sucked, are actually — we come to see this — the obverse of the same force: dependency, the fear of being bereft. Both aspects are located in the object of love. Hence the terrible and pitiful conflict with Miriam, and the overall sense of tragic inevitability.

The sense of what is 'fixed and stable' as against what is 'emptiness, almost like a vacuum', and the sense of what is behind and comforting, and what is in front and threatening, all this comes into focus as the circle of lamplight. The great locus is in chapter IV, 'The young Life of Paul'. At this point in the novel Paul is established as the main centre of consciousness, so that the feelings are importantly his; but what is now given us as his childish perception, including dread, is part of the symphonic texture of the whole.

The family moves to 'a house on the brow of the hill, commanding a view of the valley, which spread out like a convex cockle shell, or a clamp shell, before it. In front of the house was a huge old ash-tree. The west wind ... caught the houses with full force, and the tree shrieked again' (84).

The first development of this set of themes is as recollection by the child of his parents' quarrels at night: the two voices in anger, the banging of his father's fist on the table:

The winter of their first year in the new house, their father was very bad. The children played in the street, on the brim of the wide dark valley, until eight o'clock. Then they went to bed. Their mother sat sewing below. Having such a great space in front of the house gave the children a feeling of night, of vastness, and of terror. This terror came in from the shrieking of the tree and the anguish of the home discord. (84)

Space, night, vastness, terror are equated, and given a voice in the tree. This is what threatens to burst in with William's coffin. Psychic structures are being built up, the parents' conflict being translated in the child's consciousness into constitutive elements of his world:

He [Morel] might hit their mother again. There was a feeling of horror, a kind of bristling in the darkness, and a sense of blood. They lay with their hearts in the grip of an intense anguish ... And then, came the horror of the sudden silence ... was it a silence of blood? (85)

The children then hear another noise, the drumming of water into the kettle, being put ready for the morning. So it is all right; they can go to sleep in peace. There follows an equally central experience, at first summarily encapsulated: 'So they were happy in the morning, happy, very happy, playing, dancing at night round the lonely lamppost in the midst of the darkness' (85).

A few paragraphs later follows the unpacking of this notation. It begins with an essential prelude: 'In the winter nights, when it was cold, and grew dark early, Mrs Morel would put a brass candlestick on the table, light a tallow candle to save the gas. The children finished their bread and butter, or dripping, and were ready to go out to play' (85). Lawrence establishes that, outside,

The lamp-lighter came along ... Darkness shut down over the valley, work was gone, it was night.
    Then Paul ran anxiously into the kitchen. The one candle still burned on the table, the big fire glowed red, Mrs Morel sat alone. (86)

Once that security inside is established, the important ritual of playing out of doors is taken up again and completed: by now we have learned to give words like 'hollow' and 'space', 'darkness' and 'night' their due weight:

The entry was very dark, and at the end, the whole great night opened out, in a hollow, with a little tangle of lights below ... The farthest tiny lights seemed to stretch out the darkness forever. The children looked anxiously down the road at the one lamp-post, which stood at the end of the field path. If the little, luminous space were deserted, the two boys felt genuine desolation. They stood with their hands in their pockets under the lamp, turning their backs on the night ... (101)

When they are joined, even by one other, play begins. 'There was only this one lamp-post. Behind, was the great scoop of darkness, as if all the night were there.' I have listed the uses of the word 'scoop'. If we look back to the description of the house, with the valley 'like a convex cockle shell, or a clamp shell, before it', we reflect that a big clam-shell can be used as a scoop. The sense of something eroding or digging away what one stands on is thematic.

Sometimes the children would fight,

... hate with a fury of hatred, and flee home in terror. Paul never forgot, after one of these fierce internecine fights, seeing a big red moon lift itself up, slowly, between the waste road over the hill-top; steadily, like a great bird. And he thought of the bible, that the moon should be turned to blood ... And then the wild, intense games went on again under the lamp post, surrounded by so much darkness. Mrs Morel ... would hear the children singing away ...

They sounded so perfectly absorbed in the game, as their voices came out of the night, that they had the feel of wild creatures singing. It stirred the mother. And she understood when they came in at eight o'clock, ruddy, with brilliant eyes, and quick passionate speech.

They all loved the ... house for its openness, for the great scallop of the world it had in view. (101–2)

That last sentence has operated a transformation, to a daylight security. The previous night is exciting, but the fragile security it offers is based on the correspondence between the lonely lamppost outside and the lonely candle on the kitchen table within. The lamp is behind one as one faces the vast hollow of the night, as in the dangerous home where the mother is the only complete security. Feeling safe outside, the children undergo a fairy-story transformation into wild creatures, natural denizens of the night. The moon, turned to blood, is a portent; the quarrel between the children shows that there is in them the same thing that makes the parents quarrel, to produce a silence of blood. The great ash-tree speaks to them of horror outside even when they are in bed. Out there is 'night', 'space'. All the family are aware of this, even in small matters; when the parents wait for William's train to arrive at Christmas 'They were both a bit cross with each other, so gnawed with anxiety. The ash-tree moaned outside in a cold, raw wind. And all that space of night from London home!' (105).

Much force has therefore accumulated behind those words and the figure of the ash-tree in the culminating scene where William's coffin is brought into the living-room; the night is no longer held at bay outside the circle of light, has invaded the home at last; all the feared and destructive forces in the family find their equivalent in the world out there.

And not only the house is as it were permeable to this force. There is an extraordinary moment in chapter VIII, 'Strife in Love', where the jealous opposition between Mrs Morel and Miriam has been identified, and the mother has had the thought about Miriam 'sucking him up'. Paul is aware of it, and is, without understanding why, cruel to Miriam. Coming home at night from a walk with Miriam, he is 'wild with torture'. 'Then, brought up against a stile, he stood for some minutes and did not move' (a foreshadowing of his very same posture in the very last paragraphs of the book).

There was a great hollow of darkness fronting him, and on the black upslopes, patches of tiny lights, and in the lowest trough of the night, a flare of the pit. It was all weird and dreadful. Why was he torn so ... If Miriam caused his mother suffering then he hated her ... Why did she make him feel as if he were uncertain of himself, insecure, an indefinite thing, as if he had not sufficient sheathing to prevent the night and the space breaking into him? (231)

It is an extraordinary perception; it inverts the sense of being sucked out of oneself into a sense of being invaded by the other. But these heads-and-tails transpositions are a familiar psychological mechanism. There is logic in it; if there are two terms in a polarity, one automatically calls up the other, just because it is an opposite. So in the novel white light and gold, pressure-lamp and candle, moon and sun, mother and father, safety and danger, firm ground and space, suction and pressure, night and day – each calls up the other, and they are all linked by being the binary elements of one mental world. However, if you attempt, as I have just done, to place the elements in a consistent order, you find that you can't carry it right through.

Paul even grows into a certain familiarity with his own associations; since he is an artist, he must: without being too conscious of them, he must be able to use them. In the scene with Clara where he drops flowers onto her hair he also draws her attention to the way the bluebells have strayed outside the wood. It triggers one of the polarities: the circle inside which you feel safe, or the circle you press into as outsider. He says 'It makes me think of the wild men of the woods, how terrified they would be when they got breast to breast with the open space.' (So, they are like him, perhaps.) He goes on to wonder which was more frightened, those 'bursting out of their darkness of woods upon all the space of light, or those from the open tip-toeing into the forests'. She thinks the second, and he agrees, so finding her interestingly different, thus not like his mother and Miriam: 'Yes, you *do* feel like one of the open space sort – trying to force yourself into the dark ...' (279–80).

The sense of permeability leads forward to the final development of this set of motifs in the last chapter, 'Derelict'. At the end of the previous chapter Paul is able to make some kind of sense of his situation, but one can feel the 'prose' sense slipping towards the imagery of unconscious states:

His mother had really supported his life. He had loved her, they two had in fact faced the world together. Now she was gone, and forever behind him was the gap in life, the tear in the veil, through which his life seemed to drift slowly, as if he were drawn towards death. He wanted someone, of their own free initiative, to help him. (451)

Again, the sense of what is, or is not 'behind', supporting. In the absence of that support a vacuum is set up, and he will be sucked out of life unless someone will hold on to him. Now it is his mother's influence doing what she had accused

Miriam of doing; but Miriam has not the force to lay hold of him, and say 'You are mine'; she proves this in the last scene together: 'She could only sacrifice herself to him, sacrifice herself every day, gladly. And that he did not want' (461–2). So he is left in the metaphysical horror where the whole world shares his insecurity:

> There seemed no reason why people should go along the street, and houses pile up in the daylight. There seemed no reason why these things should occupy the space, instead of leaving it empty ...
> ... The first snowdrops came. He saw the tiny drop-pearls among the grey. They would have given him the liveliest emotion at one time. Now, they were there, but they did not seem to mean anything. In a few moments they would cease to occupy that place, and just the space would be where they had been ...
> The realest thing was the thick darkness at night. That seemed to him whole and comprehensible and restful. He could leave himself to it. (454–5)

This projection, his sense of a cosmic night, a limitless space in which things exist for a moment and are gone has now no countervailing power: he has an impulse to abandon himself to this drift towards death, as if it were a physical force:

> When he turned away, he felt the last hold for him had gone. The town, as he sat upon the car, stretched away, over the bay of railway, a level fume of lights. Beyond the town the country, little smouldering spots for more towns – the sea – the night – on and on! And he had no place in it. Whatever spot he stood on, there he stood alone. From his breast, from his mouth sprang the endless space – and it was there behind him, everywhere. The people hurrying along the streets offered no obstruction to the void in which he found himself. (463–4)

As the passage continues, 'void' recurs; it links with 'firmament', to remind us of Genesis, that in the beginning the earth was without form, and void; and God who said, Let there be light, divided the waters above from the waters below by a firmament. So now creation is being unmade; we are back with darkness on the face of the deep. Lawrence is here invoking both Paul's Bible knowledge and his reading in the popular scientific literature of his day, using the notion of a mechanical universe running down to cancel the hope implicit in the creation-myth. There is also a vertiginous sense of relativity, developed from what has been said in previous pages about the occupation of space by transitory objects and people: it now offers a brief delusive sense of continued contact with the mother, but this too is a temptation towards death:

They were small shadows whose footsteps and voices could be heard, but in each of them, the same night, the same silence. He got off the car. In the country all was dead still. Little stars shone high up, little stars spread far away in the floodwaters, a firmament below. Everywhere the vastness and terror of the immense night which is roused and stirred for a brief while by the day, but which returns, and will remain at last eternal, holding everything in its silence and its living gloom. There was no Time, only Space. Who could say his mother had lived and did not live? She had been in one place, and was in another, that was all. And his soul could not leave her, wherever she was. Now she was gone abroad into the night, and he was with her still. They were together.

He comes back from this vacancy, reminded, by the physical resistance of a real object, that he too is real and here: as so often in Lawrence, a character sees his own hands and is reminded that he is this body, and it goes into space with these extensions, like tendrils:

But yet there was his body, his chest that leaned against the stile, his hands on the wooden bar. They seemed something. Where was he? – one tiny upright speck of flesh, less than an ear of wheat lost in the field.

There is another Biblical reminiscence here; 'Verily, verily, I say unto you, Except a corn of wheat fall into the ground and die, it abideth alone: but if it die, it bringeth forth much fruit' (John 12.24). But this is not a temptation to suicide, it is, as in the Gospel, a demand for a rebirth. The equation with 'flesh' is a transubstantiation-image. Here is lodged our sense that the ending of the novel is not purely negative. But we have to face the depth of the despair from which Paul has to return:

He could not bear it. On every side the immense dark silence seemed pressing him, so tiny a speck [previous texts read spark; but Lawrence is pursuing his covert corn-image] into extinction, and yet, almost nothing, he could not be extinct. Night, in which everything was lost, went reaching out, beyond stars and sun. Stars and sun, a few bright grains, went spinning round for terror and holding each other in embrace, there in a darkness that outpassed them all and left them tiny and daunted.

There is a reference-back, there, to the scene of love-making with Clara in the field where the peewits screamed. This is a positive which Lawrence has worked hard to establish, against the grain of the book as a whole. Clara's eyes, we remember, were 'dark and shining and strange, life wild at the source staring into his life' (398). He and she had met like Adam and Eve, who 'realised the magnificence of the power which drove them out of Paradise and across the great night and the great day of humanity ... To know their own nothingness, to know the tremendous living flood which carried them always, gave them rest within themselves' (398). It had been an intimation which only he had felt, and it was vulnerable. Clara on the Lincolnshire beach reminded him of the other kind of 'grain'; she had been 'lost like a grain of sand in the beach – just a concentrated speck blown along – a tiny white foam-bubble – almost nothing among the morning' (402). But then again, in his love-making with her,

His hands were like creatures, living; his limbs, his body were all life and consciousness, subject to no will of his, but living in themselves. Just as he was, so it seemed the vigorous, wintry stars were strong also with life. He and they struck with the same pulse of fire. And the same joy of strength which held the bracken-frond stiff near his eyes held his own body firm. It was if he and the stars and the dark herbage and Clara were licked up in an immense tongue of flame which tore onwards and upwards. (408)

That momentary, intensely positive sense of the cosmic purpose has, as consciousness, been turned into its negative inversion at the end, yet survives subliminally as the instinct to survive:

So much, and himself, infinitesimal, at the core a nothingness, and yet not nothing.
  'Mother!' he whimpered, 'mother!'

She was the only thing that held him up, himself, amid all this. And she was gone, intermingled herself! He wanted her to touch him, have him alongside with her.

Here is the exact parallel with the scene at the end of Part I. But here 'alongside with her' can only mean the grave, and he wants to live.

But no, he would not give in. Turning sharply, he walked towards the city's gold phosphorescence. His fists were shut, his mouth set fast. He would not take that direction, to the darkness, to follow her. He walked towards the faintly humming, glowing town, quickly. (464)

'Gold' has become an important word, associated with the candle-flame, with the sun, with pollen and with honey. These elements are combined by bees, and the town is humming, like a beehive, glowing with its lamplights.

If we have a question at the end of the book, it is, given the history we have followed, *can* Paul Morel successfully break free of that past? I think the implicit answer is yes, and that we can say this because of our sense of the meaning of another set of themes, to do with sacrifice. What Miriam offers in their last interview is sacrifice, of herself, and once more that is rejected. To trace this theme we have to go back to the beginning.

When he leaves home, William burns all his love letters, with a strange joy ('Soon there was a heap of twisted black pages, all that remained of the file of scented letters', 81). The sense that the girls themselves have been annihilated is curiously confirmed when we turn the page to the next chapter and come on the episode where Paul sacrifices the doll Arabella. It belongs to Annie, and one day he jumps on it and breaks it by accident. Annie 'sat down to weep a dirge'. Paul feels guilty but unrepentant. 'So long as Annie wept for the doll he sat helpless with misery.' He is so upset that she forgives him. A day or two afterwards she is shocked:

'Let's make a sacrifice of Arabella,' he said. 'Let's burn her.' ... He made an altar of bricks, pulled some of the shavings out of Arabella's body, put the waxen fragments into the hollow face ...

and set the whole thing alight ... So long as the stupid big doll burned, he rejoiced in silence. At the end, he poked among the embers with a stick, fished out the arms and legs, all blackened, and smashed them under stones.

'That's the sacrifice of Missis Arabella,' he said. 'An' I'm glad there's nothing left of her.'

Which disturbed Annie inwardly, although she could say nothing. He seemed to hate the doll so intensely, because he had broken it. (82–3)

So guilt may go up in the smoke of the sacrifice. It is a curious psychic mechanism, used against people one has injured. You purge your guilt by taking revenge on the thing or person who makes you feel guilty, and their annihilation frees you. It seems immoral, but is a kind of fierce morality and is the ethical residue of the book: offer up your guilt and be free of it; do not accept even a loving bondage. Be free. Others will try to make you what they want you to be: refuse, and become yourself.

The idea of sacrifice is most obviously associated with Miriam: the actual word is used many times in connection with her; she is a willing victim, a martyr. But Mrs Morel has made her sacrifices too; the opposition between the two women reveals what they have in common: their intensity, their spirituality, their love for Paul, which is both noble and subtly possessive: all this is mediated through the image of the white light, which generates the associated words 'clenched' and 'gripped'. The one passes into the other in that the loving woman is clenched around her love, but what she loves she grips. That in turn generates the sense that she draws out the soul of whatever or whoever she loves; and by a strange insight this is conveyed in Miriam's habit of taking things to her lips, as if to draw them into her or, in Mrs Morel's word, literally to suck the soul out. She does this with flowers too; 'Why must you always be fondling things,' Paul bursts out. It is 'as if you wanted to pull the heart out of them ... You wheedle the soul out of things ... always begging things to love you' (257).

There are two scenes where Paul too eats flowers, and this gives a strange twist to the theme of sacrifice. The first is a slight notation; Paul is in the fields with Clara and Miriam; the way they all look at the flowers and pick them reflects their natures. 'What right have you to pull them?' Clara asks; and he says 'Because I like them, and want them.' Miriam thinks they must be treated with reverence. Paul says 'Yes ... But no, you get 'em because you want them.' He eats 'the little yellow trumpets' (278–9). He is assertive and contrary, where Miriam is sensitive, perhaps because she is. But in the later scene, with his mother, we sense a link with the great night-pieces, and a profound intended symbolism.

He has, between the two flower-scenes, insisted on a sexual relationship with Miriam, and she has submitted to the sacrifice.

Suddenly she gripped her arms round him, and clenched her body stiff.

'You *shall* have me,' she said through her shut teeth. (327)

Then she would submit, religiously, to the sacrifice. He should have her. And at the thought her whole body clenched itself involuntarily, hard, as if against something. (328)

... it was a sacrifice, in which she felt something of horror. (330)

The sacrifice produces a sense of death in him, as if he is in a night-realm: the drift towards death, the sense of being sucked out of life is initiated by this failure. It is another profound imagining:

To him now life seemed a shadow, day a white shadow, night, and death, and stillness, and inaction, this seemed like *being*. To be alive, to be urgent, and insistent, that was *not-to-be*. The highest of all was, to melt out into the darkness and sway there, identified with the great Being. (331)

We can feel the link forward with the final scene. One thing which makes us feel that he will come back from that night is the basic unconscious self-assertion of the flowers-at-night scene I have mentioned, where, like his mother at the very beginning of the book, he goes into the real actual night and comes back with something. But where she, having smiled at it, brushed it off, he eats it (the flesh of this sacrifice once given) before he spits it out. The link between the scenes is given by the Annunciation-flowers:

It grew late. Through the open door, stealthily, came the scent of madonna lilies, almost as if it were prowling abroad. Suddenly he got up and went out of doors.

The beauty of the night made him want to shout. A half moon, dusky gold, was sinking behind the black sycamore at the end of the garden, making the sky dull purple with its glow. Nearer, a dim white fence of lilies went across the garden, and the air all round seemed to stir with scent, as if it were alive. He went across the bed of pinks, whose keen perfume came sharply across the rocking, heavy scent of the lilies, and stood alongside the white barrier of flowers. They flagged all loose, as if they were panting. The scent made him drunk. He went down to the field to watch the moon sink under.

A corn-crake in the hay-close called insistently. The moon slid quite quickly downwards, growing more flushed. Behind him, the great flowers leaned as if they were calling. And then, like a shock, he caught another perfume, something raw and coarse. Hunting round, he found the purple iris, touched their fleshy throats, and their dark, grasping hands. At any rate he had found something. They stood stiff in the darkness. Their scent was brutal. The moon was melting down upon the crest of the hill. It was gone, all was dark. The corncrake called still.

Breaking off a pink he suddenly went indoors ...

He stood with the pink against his lips.

'I shall break off with Miriam, mother,' he answered calmly.

(337−8)

After an exchange with his mother the scene closes:

'On Sunday I break off,' he said, smelling the pink. He put the flower in his mouth. Unthinking, he bared his teeth, closed them on the blossom slowly, and had a mouthful of petals. These he spat into the fire, kissed his mother, and went to bed. (338)

It is easy to see how the pink is like Miriam; he has eaten her up, and now is going to spit her out. It follows that the iris-scent represents the 'passion' which he goes to Clara to find. As for the lilies in the 'dusky gold' moonlight, they resist easy equivalences, but perhaps they are an annunciation of an ultimate perfect desire, the flower of the rebirth one must always be willing to undergo. Lawrence rejected the cult of crucifixion as God's imagined self-sacrifice. For him it was the incarnation and resurrection that represented the divine power to go on into a new life on this earth.

A psychoanalytical approach to the case-history of Paul Morel would lead one to see that the mother's influence had made it difficult for him to love any woman in a whole-hearted way. At one point this is even stated, or half-stated in an extraordinary way which comes up to the problem, but does not fully face it, so replicating Paul's struggling half-consciousness:

> He looked round. A good many of the nicest men he knew were like himself, bound in by their own virginity, which they could not break out of. They were so sensitive to their women, that they would go without them for ever rather than do them a hurt, an injustice. Being the sons of mothers whose husbands had blundered rather brutally through their feminine sanctities, they were themselves too diffident and shy. They could easier deny themselves than incur any reproach from a woman. For a woman was like their mother, and they were full of the sense of their mother. (323)

Of course, Paul does nonetheless blunder rather brutally through the feminine sanctities of both Miriam and Clara, thus following his father, for all his dissociation from him. Where he finds his mother replicated in Miriam, there is a powerful attraction for that very reason, and for the other reason that Miriam fosters his creativity, or his consciousness of it. He does something similar for her, so that their hyper-consciousness, a powerful faculty which transcends mere intelligence, is mutually reinforcing, and they give each other an extraordinary education of the feelings – within limits. But a sexual relationship with her, which his consciousness demands and her consciousness requires her to give him, is felt by both as a deathly process. One might say that this is because subconsciously he feels he is making love to a woman too like his mother, and her jealousy provides endorsement of this. The sense of 'death' and 'night' in this sexuality makes it repugnant; at the conscious level he sees this as the thing in Miriam which, even in passion, requires him always to be aware of her as person and him as other person, that unremitting consciousness. What he finds with Clara is a rest from that consciousness, but the conventional psychological account would say it is a 'split-off' or merely sexual relationship. So far as that is the case, it justifies Clara's charge that he is not 'there' in the relationship; he wants 'it' rather than her. Yet in that affair too there is a powerful echo of his parents' relationship, but this time he is displacing a man like his father. He is able to restore the couple to each other, but that requires him to leave.

In the end, what he is left with seems to be just the basic biological instinct: he will live on. The deeper positive, the Annunciation which the book hints at throughout, the possibility of a good sexual love, which would not be split off from a good way of living in the world, is not found by the two main protagonists of the younger generation. To Miriam Paul expresses it as the peace of shedding one's personal will, but the paradox is that he has to formulate this wish, which comes from the will, the intelligence, as an idea. With Clara it is his intuition of going, for one moment, with the movement of the whole universe; but the mechanical attempt to repeat that rapture comes from the will again, and denatures the experience.

The crucial night- or twilight-scenes, which every reader finds remarkable, are like repeated glimpses of a realm of otherness which you can enter if you are overtaken by a moment's unconsciousness, and can then hear and see. This is like a recovered knowledge or wisdom, or the original religious sense which underlies formal creeds. That recovery is the personal need of the representative individual, Paul, as conveyed through the logic of the story. It shows the ways in which the individual in this century needs to be returned to a sense of being in the world, and how much one is prevented by the burden of consciousness stereotyped by social living.

Mrs Morel has her inkling of this lost harmony when, dazzled by her young husband-to-be, she sees his 'sensuous flame of life', and it 'seemed to her something wonderful, beyond her'. Her tragedy is that she neither recognises nor holds on to the vision. Paul's tragedy is that he has the openness, but the vision is inflected, even distorted, by his personal situation, his conflict. But how could it be otherwise, for anyone else? Everyone has to start there, in their own subjectivity, with their own problems. That is why the story is representative: 'the tragedy of thousands of young men in England' – and everywhere.

To the rationalising sceptic it must seem an odd thing to say, but the whole book gives it a sense: what Paul needs is dusky-golden, warm, like candle-light. This is his father's realm, and he has shut off his father and needs to find him again. What he inherits from his mother lures him towards the white light of consciousness, 'baffled and gripped' into incandescence. He needs this too, because it turns his spontaneousness into consciousness, especially in his art; but, pursued exclusively, it is pathological, even deathly. His task is to counterbalance the two elements of his inheritance; and he sets off 'quickly' towards what his instinct sees as warm and glowing and faintly humming.

That, the whole book suggests, is part of a wider search. Metaphor is the language which expresses the less conscious, more instinctive movements of the psyche. The child is peculiarly open to these movements, even a prey to them. If Paul Morel feels that constant sense of the lighted circle, which centres on his mother, and contrasts it with the emptiness, the vacuum, of the surrounding night, space, the void, it is a mistake to write this off as a childish fear. It is a childish truth. The twenty-six-year-old author feels the same dread when his mother is taken from him and his love-affairs have collapsed. His task is not to repudiate his psychic history, to neutralise his metaphors by explaining them, but to take them as a way of moving more freely in and around his world. He may find he is able to transcend the circle, to become what he calls 'one of the open space sort', or to recognise that the threatening other must be invited in, since it may be what Lawrence later called the dark god.

Metaphor conveys without conceptualising an immediate sense of being in the world, where one thing is laid alongside, or takes the place of another. This is a kind of meaning personal to the utterer, avoiding statement, but the attempt to say what *Sons and Lovers* is about leads inevitably to interpretation. The polarity of white light and golden light seems to oppose the mind, the consciousness − what we do actually project − to another way of being which precedes knowing. Since the Renaissance, the problem of knowing has been that the consciousness is by its own operation cut off from what it knows, and the harder it tries to know, the more cut off it is. To be in the world and not to be so cut off from it may now be impossible, especially if we set ourselves to do it as a conscious project. Lawrence can however dramatise the predicament, and promote a search for a way out; his work suggests that if there is a possibility of going round by another route or actually bridging the gap, it would be through an art which starts from a deep spontaneity and proceeds by constantly returning to it. We want, need, to be, in the end, conscious of what it brings; but to imagine the original state, to delay the operation of consciousness, and to make it also conscious of its own deforming power is – inescapable paradox – a great addition to its range.

The moments of vision: of the moonlit garden, the sunset, the moment of the rosebush, the scent of iris, the sound of the peewits calling, moments which are given to Gertrude Morel and her son Paul and to Miriam Leivers, with their recurrent hint of an Annunciation, can be read as no more than a distraction-fit, a mood, a projection, a psychic oddity. At that level the sceptical modern reader can write them off as mere poetry. One goes a level deeper by invoking the psychoanalytical explanation, which makes personal feeling echo a need which comes from further back, but leaves things at that level of the family drama. Admittedly, that opens up perspectives pointed to by Sophocles, Shakespeare, Ibsen and Freud; but Lawrence also wanted the religious dimension which came naturally to his predecessors but now had to be recovered.

Any religious vision is vulnerable, Lawrence knew, to the sceptical response that it is a mere projection, a subjective pseudo-answer to a personal predicament or a general social problem. A more sympathetic response might say that the metaphors are powerful, and do convey valuable feelings, which of course we respect, but religious feeling in this century can be no more than metaphor. But if this is true now, it always was; the language of religious feeling has to be analogical, moving from human experience outward to its boundary.

To recognise this is not to dispose either of the feeling or the mode of utterance. How else can you speak of the other?

T. S. Eliot meditated the same problem more than a quarter of a century later when he wrote *Four Quartets*; 'The Dry Salvages' uses remarkably similar insights:

> For most of us, there is only the unattended
> Moment, the moment in and out of time,
> The distraction fit, lost in a shaft of sunlight,
> The wild thyme unseen, or the winter lightning
> Or the waterfall, or music heard so deeply
> That it is not heard at all, but you are the music
> While the music lasts. These are only hints or guesses ...

But Eliot goes on, and seems, to many readers, to force the issue:

> The hint half guessed, the gift half understood, is Incarnation.
> (*Complete Poems and Plays*, 1969, p. 190)

That turns the hint half guessed into a conviction, with the implication that a whole system of doctrines follows. Lawrence does not go that further step. He accepts that it is now as metaphor that these things must be intuited by a writer or conveyed to a reader. The modern response is both accepted and answered by Lawrence's writing. In this mode you receive his intuition, and either agree to contemplate it, or reject it — and much of Lawrence with it.

Chapter 4

The 'Foreword'

Lawrence suddenly wrote the 'Foreword' while the book was already with the publishers, sending it to Garnett with a separate postcard on 20 January 1913. On 17 January he had sent the great letter to Collings: on previous nights he had seen *Ghosts* and *Hamlet* performed in Italian in Gargnano.

Perhaps Garnett, puzzled by this strange document, asked if Lawrence really wanted it printed; in a letter of 1 February he said no, he had wanted to *write* it, not to have it printed. We can infer an operation of the demon, a spontaneity, which had presented him with something he had not expected; or perhaps it had been like a sketch, an experiment in a new mode of writing, which he might or might not take further.

In fact he did. The 'Foreword' inaugurates his whole vein of philosophical writings, and they can be seen as successive rewritings of this first attempt. Many readers are familiar with his later statement in another 'Foreword', the one written for *Fantasia of the Unconscious* (1922):

This pseudo-philosophy of mine − 'pollyanalytics,' as one of my respected critics might say − is deduced from the novels and the poems, not the reverse. The novels and poems come unwatched out of one's pen. And then the absolute need which one has for some sort of satisfactory mental attitude towards oneself and things in general makes one try to abstract some general conclusions from one's experiences as a writer and as a man. The novels and poems are pure passionate experience. These 'pollyanalytics' are inferences made afterwards, from the experience.

The novel was indeed written first, and the 'Foreword' does attempt to extract conclusions from it − strange ones if you are not aware of the religious dimension. But it reads as if it too came unwatched out of the pen and was a surprise to the author as well as to us; it is not easier to understand than the novel — rather the reverse — and it is itself a text which Lawrence obsessively rewrote. This happened first in *Study of Thomas Hardy* in Autumn 1914, then in 'The Crown' (1915; heavily revised in 1925), then in *Twilight in Italy* (1916), then in two lost rewritings called 'Goats and Compasses' (1916) and 'At the Gates' (1917), as well as in a surviving work 'The Reality of Peace' (1917). That led into the several times redrafted *Studies in Classic American Literature*, finally published in 1923, and this in turn leads into the later writings with a psycho-physiological orientation. The final statements are the posthumous *Sketches of Etruscan Places* (1932), which at one point even uses actual words from the 'Foreword', and *Apocalypse* (0931), which gives a last statement about being 'breast to breast with the cosmos'. All these writings are linked by continuous threads of preoccupation, expressed characteristically in repeated and related images; and it is not fanciful to think of them as attempts to get out something which had always been there, waiting to be reached, but also receding and changing like the rainbow — what Leavis called the 'ungrasped apprehended'.

The 'Foreword' was not published in Lawrence's lifetime; for many years it was only available in Aldous Huxley's one-volume selection of Lawrence's letters, published in 1932. Now that it is at last attached to the novel, in a corrected text, in the Cambridge edition, we can begin to make sense of it in relation to the novel, and see it as inaugurating this series of other related writings.

The 'Foreword' has two elements; a vein of Biblical or prophetic utterance in which Christian or Old Testament terms are used in a very assertive style which conceals the fact that the terms are being given new meanings; and a vein of free metaphorical fantasy using flower- and bee-images.

My guess is that Lawrence has here crystallised a group of unstated, even unconscious, intentions. He had throughout the novel been creating a network of discreet allusions to Christian doctrines, especially to the Annunciation. Paul does also announce to Miriam the beginning of a set of beliefs which could be called pantheist, or in modern terms vitalist-theist, but not Christian. More exactly, Paul sees as divine the creative power at the heart of the universe, but he cannot see God as personal, still less as male; and this God takes no more account of the death of William than of the fall of the sparrow. Nonetheless there is a divinity in things, and in his pictures Paul attempts to capture this 'shimmering', this sense of an underlying original basic life, like protoplasm, which takes form in each individual living thing (183).

If God is not personal, the Persons of the old Christian Trinity – Father, Son and Holy Spirit – need to be redefined if they are to go on being emotional, intellectual and artistic forces, and not to lapse into dead conventional forms, picture-book images: especially the old man with the white beard and the long robe. This can only be done by metaphorising them, and this is what the 'Foreword' attempts. An example had been given by John's Gospel, Lawrence's favourite book of the Bible. Like Genesis, it begins 'In the beginning ...' – as if re-telling the Creation – but at once it de-personalises Father and Son, turning them into the Word and the Word-made-Flesh; Christ is further metaphorised, de-personalised, as light continuously shining in hostile darkness. This is a figure for the operation of the Spirit; it also supports a sense of creation as not something once and for all time, but always going on. I have suggested above how much emotion Lawrence has invested in the schema of a circle of light opposed to an endless voracious space, the void before creation, the vacuum.

So, in the last Gospel, Father and Son have become polarities, not persons. But if Lawrence were to take recent thought into consideration, especially Herbert Spencer's huge effort to take Darwinian evolutionary theory into an overarching social-historical framework, he would have perceived that evolution departs from the unindividuated, the homogeneous, and moves towards the individuated, the heterogeneous. Only individuals, persons, can utter words, so the Word itself cannot be the origin. Unindividuated life, the origin, protoplasm, must be Flesh. So the order in John (first Word, then Flesh) must be inverted, the old scheme turned on its head. That lends itself to a witty treatment, and had better be treated so, if it is not to seem heavy and blasphemous to literal-minded believers. But it remains serious, since it both divinises the evolutionary scheme and gives a new lease of life to the old terms.

Another subversive twist is given by the obvious thought that woman is the fountain of all flesh because women give birth to men. Moreover modern biological thought tells us that maleness is a differentiation, so that life in its original undifferentiated form is female. If you are thinking that the primal source is the Father, you have to add 'more properly, the Mother'. Hence what seems like a little joke in the 'Foreword', which was no joke to the author of *Sons and Lovers.*

Lawrence also plays on another reminiscence of Biblical terms, the 'one flesh' which in the marriage service symbolises union. In Genesis the myth that Eve was made from Adam's rib suggests that in marriage the two sexes are as it were re-united, undoing that separation. In Matthew 19, Jesus refers to the myth, and to the words of Genesis, in instituting Christian marriage ('What therefore God hath joined together, let no man put asunder'). This too has to be reformulated: married people may want to be one flesh, but it does not happen because a service is performed and a certificate signed.

The Flesh, the Father, is too far back, too inaccessible, has no face, no individuality. We only have access to it through the Word, that is, in the individuals we are ourselves, and find ourselves among: and they are expressed as what they do or say. We can only take them at that level, of their individuality. But this is something which many cannot achieve. In the words of the letter to Collings, we are unable to *be*, and drop into 'forms of not-being', such as humanitarianism, where we worry about our neighbour's social status. Here Lawrence is glancing at the Sermon on the Mount, and the command to love one's neighbour as oneself. He sees it as a temptation to think of one's neighbour as *like* oneself; hence to love oneself. Freud saw this as the narcissistic origin of compassion. Lawrence went on thinking about this, and came to accept Jesus's other formulation of the commandment: 'Love your enemy.' If you see that your enemy, as a law of his nature, may want to kill you, you are not tempted to think of him as like yourself. Rather, you see him and yourself as parts of a nature which includes predation and may require you to defend yourself. This happens to Paul Morel: 'And if he [Dawes] kills you?' says Clara (390). He has to accept the possibility, and Dawes nearly does it.

In a more freely-moving second section, Lawrence drops the Biblical terms and follows a flower-metaphor. This uses the whole cycle, seed-sprout-plant-flower-seed, to represent the essential creative process which derives from the unknowable Father, the origin from which all individual acts of creativity or procreation flow, and who is expressed as Word in these acts. Only in that way can he utter. The flower chosen as ideal blossoming is the rose, traditional emblem of perfection for Christian mystics.

The third section generalises from the first two. We know the Father, the unknowable, only 'in the Flesh, in Woman. She is the door for our in-going and our out-coming. In her we go back to the Father ...' (471). This is the ideal love-relationship, marriage, which has not been realised in the novel; it is here announced as if it were a programme for a future novel, and the Biblical phrases about the door-keeper look forward to their use again in *The Rainbow*. Lawrence goes on to make strikingly absolute claims for woman in this relationship; the flower-image generates a bee-image, and woman is the queen-bee: 'for she lies at the centre of the hive, and stands in the way of bees for God the Father ... In her all things are born ...' He goes further: woman is 'in herself, whether she will have it or not, God the Father'. Men come and go, to the hive and back, in their daily work, their creativity. They are sustained in this by their relationship with the woman; so far as they are husbands this must mean a sexual relationship. The figure is both apt and ambiguous in that all bees are born of the queen, and are sons; they do revolve around her and the hive; they do in the end fertilise her, are therefore sons and lovers.

Lawrence comes back to this enigma at the end; but first he wants to derive a figure of harmonious work, which can be transfigured into real creativity. The ordinary worker, with a good marriage, comes and goes to and from the home, and his wife sustains him sexually. The image of ordinary work in the 'Foreword' is carpentry; since Christ was supposed to have been born into a carpenter's family, we have a reminder of the Holy Family as archetypal, and also as ordinary.

But all work is in some sense a 'waste', is mere excess, the throwing off of the moment's creativity, in a blossoming. The plant exists to blossom: the fact that it then produces seed is not the point, merely the result. So work, children, even art, are not the aim of life; the point is the process, the glory, which produces them, which seems to puritans mere show and to utilitarians mere 'waste'. This is obscure or implicit in the 'Foreword'; I am using the rewriting, in *Study of Thomas Hardy*, to gloss the first full expression of the theme. But the 'Foreword' does reach the cardinal doctrine: in the moment of expression, of creation, the unique identity is created or confirmed; this is what it is to *be*; one is saying 'I am I.' This 'glad cry when we know, is the Holy Ghost the Comforter' (472). One thinks again of the letter to Collings.

But this is a hope for the future. The 'Foreword' ends on a bleaker note, which looks back to the past, the parent-novel, and the failures at its heart. It considers the case 'if the man deny, or be too weak' – not, we notice, if the woman rejects or is too strong. The woman must find another man and he another woman; if the law does not permit it, then he will destroy himself, perhaps with drink, and she may turn to a son and make him her 'lover in part only ... The old son-lover was Œdipus. The name of the new one is legion.' The harm will go on being done, 'and his wife in her despair shall hope for sons, that she may have her lover in her hour' (473). The 'Foreword' seems to leave the novel where it seems to end, without explicit hope; but it is beginning to elaborate the language in which its successor-novels and the later philosophical works take up the account.

Chapter 5

Its place in literature and in Lawrence's work

A European reader would no doubt see *Sons and Lovers* as a *Bildungsroman* – a novel about youth, the education of the feelings and the formation of an identity – or as a *Kunstlerroman*, a novel about the formation of an artist. The great model is Goethe's *Wilhelm Meister*, and – through Carlyle and G.H. Lewes – Goethe was a powerful figure in late nineteenth-century England. But the native English variant, the childhood-novel with strong autobiographical overtones, is inaugurated by Dickens in *David Copperfield* (1850), Borrow in *Lavengro* (1851) and *The Romany Rye* (1857) and George Eliot in *The Mill on the Floss* (1860). We know, from Jessie Chambers's account, that Lawrence read all four. Of *David Copperfield*, she says that Lawrence felt an affinity with its hero (ET 95); and that he 'adored' *The Mill on the Floss* (ET 97). Of Borrow,

He said that [he] had mingled autobiography and fiction so inextricably in *Lavengro* that the most acute critics could not be sure where the one ended and the other began. From his subtle smile I felt he was wondering whether he might not do something in the same fashion himself. (ET 110)

As usual, she is right; though the thought opens out into a prophetic comment on her own reaction to *Sons and Lovers*. But then, the opening words of *David Copperfield* and *The Mill on the Floss* convey the very similar personal involvement of both authors in the narrative voice. Dickens's enigmatic sentences lead one to think he is pointing to himself through his disguise as the alter ego who is the 'I' of the first-person narrative: 'Whether I shall turn out to be the hero of my own life, or whether that station will be held by anybody else, these pages must show. To begin my life with the beginning of my life, I record that I was born ...' George Eliot's opening scene-setting, on the banks of the Floss, seems to be by an author speaking personally about a well-loved place: '... the little river ... seems to me like a living companion, while I wander along the bank ... I remember those large dripping willows. I remember the stone bridge.' The reader comes to feel a strong identity between Maggie Tulliver and her creator. Her nostalgic tone, and Dickens's more astringent reminiscence, in both cases set the novel back in an earlier time: things are seen through a veil or glow which idealises in her case and makes grotesquely mythical in his: these are modes of telling inherent in re-entering the world of childhood. This is the case too with Jefferies' *Amaryllis at the Fair* (1887); there is a romantic, almost a fairy-tale transformation of the remembered farm and the village. In all three cases the element of realism is psychological; the re-creation of the relationship between the parents, and the consequential relationship with the children, especially the damage done to the central consciousness through whom the story is experienced. Dickens's David is taken further into adult life than the others; unable to surmount her troubles, George Eliot's Maggie dies of them. Amaryllis is remarkable in that Jefferies transposes gender in his alter ego (as Lawrence later did with some of his). She is left in a dream-like idyll, having just met a male alter ego − as if two halves have rejoined. David Copperfield makes a disastrous marriage which replicates his parents' relationship, but is rescued from it by the death of his first wife. He is then able to marry again, and live happy ever after. His hero refuses to breach orthodox morality in the way that Paul Morel does, but the novel shows some shocking instances of the double standard. Everyone about David in some way illuminates his experience by being a living comment on it.

In relation to that tradition, *Sons and Lovers* controls its nostalgia through the realism of the scene-setting and its sense of being not so far back in time from the telling. The frankness about sexual experience means that Lawrence is able, as his predecessors were not, to show how it too is affected by the psychic burden of the partners in a relationship; it is not merely a matter of freedom to describe actions, but of showing their meaning and how it is determined. The end of the whole story is left open: Paul is neither killed nor married off; one is left wondering whether he can achieve autonomy, but sensing that he is determined to try.

He is certainly not claiming that he is about 'to forge in the smithy of my soul the uncreated conscience of my race'. When Joyce wrote that last-but-one sentence of *Portrait of the Artist as a Young Man*, published three years after *Sons and Lovers*, he was making the last notation in a series where the succession of styles tells something about the evolution of the voice speaking; this may be a young man's hubris. But it also seems like a serious ambition, from an important writer who is now ready to take off. Yet the *Portrait*, like *Sons and Lovers*, cannot be dismissed as the book which its author had to write in order to be free to go on to his real work. It is an essential part of it; and we note that in *Ulysses* the early life has not been exorcised, it remains a pressing theme. The *Portrait* anz *Sons and Lovers* demand to be compared for the way in which they remain close to the originating experience of the author, while turning it into something else, into art. The other natural comparison is with Proust's enormous elaboration, where the artist's vocation is linked to the recovery of the self. The three writers, Lawrence, Joyce, Proust, also show remarkable affinities, as well as obvious differences, in the way in which they composed their work, considered as a unified whole; and this is why they require in the editors of their texts a sense of the process of constant revision through which they evolved.

That sense of the constant raid on the memory and the related creative source, so that meditation on the meaning of the experiences is inseparable from the form, often the successive forms, in which they are incorporated is greatly strengthened in Lawrence's case by situating *Sons and Lovers* in his whole work. I have already touched on the early works, preceding the novel, in which the reader can see the themes and material of *Sons and Lovers* being introduced, but handled differently, sometimes tentatively. Major early short stories, especially 'Odour of Chrysanthemums' and 'Daughters of the Vicar' in their revised forms both show a radical reworking which departs from the mother-centred view. In the first, the miner's wife's worst fear is realised: he is not late because he is in the pub; he has been killed down the pit. This causes a seismic upheaval in her consciousness; she reflects on their long marital struggle, and recognises in the body before her a man who was always unknown, whom she denied. In the second, the other wing of the diptych, a conscious young woman recognises in the body of the living man before her a strange unknown which is a wonder to her. It is as if the Morels fall in love again, but the woman is, this time, more likely to hold on to the enchantment, or turn it into something permanent, because she respects the otherness of the man.

The two next novels, *The Rainbow* and *Women in Love*, are progressions from *Sons and Lovers*. The temporal element, the succession of generations, is amplified. What Morel represents is projected back into a remoter past, of the patriarchal Brangwen men. Old Tom Brangwen is a happy Morel, secure in his life, and confirmed in his marriage to Lydia, the foreign woman with Lawrence's mother's name. This is like a serene vision; it is implied that the happiness cannot now be repeated in those terms, because they are of the past, but it represents a good which could be recreated in new terms. The second generation, of Will and Anna, is still previous to Lawrence's, but Will is given important experiences in love which correspond to Lawrence's. He represents an evolving, a more modern consciousness; the search for love seems almost successful, but then falls into a too-settled day-to-day ordinariness, an unwillingness to go further, largely because Anna loses her self in her willingness to be absorbed in motherhood. It is therefore the next generation that has to pursue the quest. Significantly, the central consciousness is a composite one; Ursula Brangwen has some of Lawrence's, some of Louie Burrows's, some of Jessie Chambers's and some of Frieda's experiences, so is representative. She is representative also in that Will, feeling rejected by Anna, turns to her and makes emotional demands on her. She has a disastrous love-affair with her cousin Skrebensky, who has something of her father in him. Her eventual chosen mate, Rupert Birkin, is first met in *Women in Love*; he is a Lawrence-figure, and she has now become a Frieda-figure. Again, there is no happy ever after. The saga ends, like *Sons and Lovers*, open into the future, but leaving a strong sense of tragedy in the failure of the relationship between Gudrun, Ursula's sister, and Gerald Crich, Birkin's friend. There is an equal determination to go on into the unknown, but no more than in *Sons and Lovers* is there an 'answer' to the inevitable problems which one's heritage has created. What is new is a self-consciousness, a power to enter into the necessary search with a directing intelligence. Given Lawrence's view about the harmful influence of consciousness and will, this is to import another set of difficulties, but there is no way of avoiding them either.

I have mentioned early short stories in which the Jessie-relationship and the Jessie-figure appear. When Jessie read *Women in Love*, she very shrewdly realised that Hermione Roddice, whom most readers identify as Lady Ottoline Morrell, is another representation of her, Jessie. The outward characteristics, the mere idiosyncrasies, are Ottoline's, but the essential disposition is Jessie's. The relationship with Miriam also lies below the surface of the final chapters of *Study of Thomas Hardy*. Readers may have been alerted by the recurrence of a haunted sense of 'the void' in earlier chapters. When we come to the retelling of *Jude the Obscure*, we find that it is a reconstitution of *Sons and Lovers*; the 'cool-lighted mind-life' that Jude and Sue lead together replicates the intellectual education Paul and Miriam give each other, their strange dependence on the spiritual illumination each derives. The book ends with a painful sense of guilt at the wrong done to Sue by Jude's forcing himself on her sexually, as an act of will. Sue was a special nature, a Cassandra or priestess-figure, with a sacred virginity vowed to the god, and this should have been respected. This has not much to do with Hardy's novel, and is surely to be seen as a transferred sense of the wrong done to Miriam. The same void provides the opening image of 'The Crown'; the succession of philosophical works written in the

War years shows Lawrence struggling with his inner forces by generalising them into universal principles. These forces include a bisexual, possibly a homosexual, component which he has to face and accept as part of his given nature.

If you look back at *The White Peacock*, the first novel, you can think of it as a first answer to the questions: 'Born where I was, when I was, to these people in this class, in England — what were the chances life offered? How was my generation advantaged or disadvantaged?' The first novel takes the group, what sociologists call the cohort, and chooses a representative, George Saxton. The observer, the narrator, is a minor figure, though we sense that he is Lawrence's alter ego, and that he has a personal problem. *Sons and Lovers* returns to that figure, and asks how the problem is representative: it is inflected by class, but created by the family, and so is both personal and universal. Later novels remain concerned with the same group, the same era, the same place. *The Rainbow* and *Women in Love* are set in the same locality, and trace the group over generations; there is now a real effort to widen the view historically and socially. People from other social classes are involved; the issue of industrialism is addressed; ultimate questions are implied, like what is this life about, what is all the effort *for*, how can people be happy in it, does that happiness reduce to employment and contentment in a conventional social marriage, or does love represent a more subversive power, in that it opens out into an unknown future which should be different?

The post-war novels are more modest in their range, but depart from the same base. Three of them, where the actual writing was interwoven, form a group. Alvina Houghton in *The Lost Girl* (started immediately after *Sons and Lovers* was finished; rvwritten 1920), Aaron Sisson in *Aaron's Rod* (begun 1917, completed 1921), Gilbert Noon in *Mr Noon* (written 1920–1) are like people Lawrence grew up with. We remember that he was going to put Alvina into *Sons and Lovers* under another name; he actually knew a Gilbert Noon, though that character is in Part I of the novel more like George Neville (the original of the friend who went to Blackpool with Paul

Morel just before Mrs Morel fell ill, and the central character of the play *The Married Man*). In Part II, first published in 1984 in the Cambridge edition of the whole novel, he is given Lawrence's own experience after leaving England in 1912.

Alvina gives this lead in the abandonment of England; she will not play the tribal mating-game, but falls in love with a foreigner who could not be more other; the wandering mountebank Ciccio who takes her off to a remote and primitive part of Italy, where she faces a new life, like that of the peasants observed in *Twilight in Italy*. Is that, actually, a better kind of marriage? What will happen to her? Who can tell?

Aaron Sisson is an interesting case in a different way. Lawrence and his immediate friends could escape Eastwood because their intelligence and their education moved them upward into the teaching profession, so they could work anywhere, and command a salary and a certain status. Aaron has to stay and embrace the other alternative; has gone down the pit, become a trade union official, married a local girl, had children. He is trapped, in the way Alvina has refused to be; he is incorporated into the local tribe; only his music, his flute, gives him a way out. One day he just goes, leaves the family, plays for a while in London, and then he too leaves England. He has an affair in Italy, but feels that the marriage tie, which he has resented, is nonetheless real. Another open question at the end of the book, which also begins to be aware of politics in Europe.

This two-part pattern: opening in the old England of the tribe, moving out to the Europe of a wider vision, but still feeling that is not the end of the matter – is repeated in *Mr Noon*. The first part is very funny in an uncomfortable way. Gilbert Noon, another teacher, is famed as a 'spooner', which is the art of going so far but not further with the girls. But he is threatened with becoming Jude the Obscure; he goes too far, is trapped, or seems so. The girl is determined to end up married to somebody, but settles for her meek fiancé. Gilbert is not so much frightened as angry at having taken part in a predetermined set of moves which might have trapped him; he determines to get out of England; resigns his post, as Lawrence did; and goes to Germany. There he meets his match, or mate, Johanna, clearly modelled on Frieda. This, it is implied, is a real marriage: not the merely social or tribal contract, but a fierce commitment which includes, requires, equally fierce struggle in order to work out a true base for a permanent relationship.

Insofar as it is quasi-autobiographical, *Mr Noon* is a continuation of *Sons and Lovers*. The same life-experience is being deployed in its next phase, and a related but new meaning is being found. It is a more hopeful book; but it was laid aside unfinished – left open in the most radical way possible. One reason why it was never finished is that Lawrence used the next phase of his own life in the chapter called 'The Nightmare' in *Kangaroo* (1923). The Lawrence-figure has now left Europe as well as England, is long-married, though the marriage has dangerous stresses. These have to do with the tension between living a life focused in the partner and the wish to be engaged in a wider life, of politics, for instance. The attractions, or temptations, of throwing in one's lot either with the extreme right or the extreme left – the choices of the 1920s and 1930s – are dramatised and rejected, and the central chapter of reminiscence shows why the trauma which Lawrence suffered in the War years 1914–18 prevents him ever again throwing in his lot with the party, the majority, the tribe, the herd. The era of corporatism, collectivism or totalitarianism could count him out. Only in a totally different society with non-European roots, the Mexico of *The Plumed Serpent*, could he imagine a new kind of wholehearted involvement – and that was a utopian dream of a total reconstitution of society, restoring the old pre-Christian religion.

So, between the experience of *Sons and Lovers* and that of *Kangaroo* there was a profoundly de-socialising experience, which means that the search for the rainbow can never again be conducted in a Western setting. This is confirmed in the last novel, *Lady Chatterley's Lover*. The hero Mellors (the name is like an inversion of Morel) is a recluse, a man who has renounced the outside world. He tells his life to Connie, and the reader is shocked to hear the Miriam-story being told again, with bitterly reductive cynicism. Some wound has turned his whole experience sour. The new love does not bring him back into the world, but it does open him to the other, as personified in the lover, and the tenderness they feel for each other is a strong but private good: the only one they can see. Connie being 'theed' and 'thoud' by Mellors is like Mrs Morel being surprised by the same convention. At the end they are going to marry, have their child and keep themselves apart from a hateful world. Lawrence completes here one task he embarked on in *Sons and Lovers*, the attempt to give words to sexual experiences. This means to treat them with proper respect, even awe. It also means, once again, to differentiate between them according to their meaning for, and what they express in the nature of, the participants. The scandal this caused confirmed him in his feeling about the world.

His first two novels were frank tragedies; in the subsequent ones, the ending is always an opening, of a sort, into the future. But the underlying feeling remains either tragic or so equivocal that one always doubts the hopefulness of the ending. But this is at the level of thought and intention, and Lawrence's main achievement is to teach us not to remain there. The thing which lies deepest of all is the sense of self-renewing life in the writing.

Bibliographical; acknowledgements

The Cambridge Edition, D H. Lawrence: *Sons and Lovers*, edited by Helen Baron and Carl Baron, Cambridge 1992, supersedes all previous printings. The Introduction and explanatory notes are very full and valuable. This study is, and all subsequent critical works must be, indebted to this work. The text is the copyright of the Estate of Frieda Lawrence Ravagli, and I am grateful for the permission of the Literary Executor, Laurence Pollinger Ltd, and Cambridge University Press for permission to quote copyright material.

The other cardinal work by Lawrence, essential to the understanding of his more formal writings, is the Letters. The volume complementary to *Sons and Lovers* is *The Letters of D.H. Lawrence, Volume I: September 1901–May 1913*, edited by James T. Boulton (Cambridge, 1979).

The standard biographical source is now John Worthen: *D.H. Lawrence: The Early Years 1885–1912* (Cambridge, 1991). This incorporates research-findings thrown up by the Cambridge Edition, itself adds substantially to the record, and is particularly exact about the differences between the life and the use made of it in the fiction. I am indebted to Worthen's work, as I am to the Barons', for my account of the background and genesis of the novel; it is important for Lawrence studies that his biography and their edition have appeared so close together and illuminate each other.

Jessie Chambers's book about the early life of Lawrence and her part in it is a classic work by a noble, intelligent and generous woman. One has to remind oneself of the courage necessary in 1935 for a middle-aged woman living in the English provinces as the quiet wife of a respected teacher to identify herself – even under a pseudonym – as the youthful lover of the notorious adulterer and pornographer Lawrence, still remembered in his birthplace and by her family and friends as a source of scandal. Her tribute to his genius, which she was first to recognise, outweighs her personal pain, and the book is full of insight. It was reissued in 1980 as *D.H. Lawrence: A Personal Record, by E.T.* (Cambridge). Her letters were collected as a special issue of the *D. H. Lawrence Review*, edited by George J. Zytaruk (Volume 12, Numbers 1–2, Spring–Summer 1979). In an important letter of 23 July 1935 to the Polish scholar W. Lutoslawski, Jessie says some things which she obviously was unable to say in her book, in a public context. The source of greatest pain to her was the title of chapter XI, 'The Test on Miriam'. Her offering herself was a pledge of love, and she had thought it mutual; to have it presented as a 'test' was a lasting wound, but not one she could say anything about to a censorious or prurient world.

The secondary literature is, after eighty years, very large, but interesting mainly to specialist scholars. A useful collection, which contains some classic essays, is the volume in the Macmillan Casebook Series, *Sons and Lovers*, edited by Gamini Salgado (1969). Notable are the early Freudian essay by the American Alfred Kuttner, published in the *Psychoanalytic Review* in 1916; Mark Schorer's 'Technique as Discovery', the origin of most subsequent criticisms of Lawrence's 'failure of impersonality'; and Dorothy van Ghent's sympathetic essay 'On *Sons and Lovers*'. Another valuable essay is Louis Martz, 'Portrait of Miriam: a Study in the Design of *Sons and Lovers*' in *Imagined Worlds: Essays on Some English Novels and Novelists in Honour of John Butt*, ed. Maynard Mack and Ian Gregor (1968), pp. 343–69.

Another collection, now out of print, but very useful, is the Penguin Critical Anthology, edited by H. Coombes (1973). It deals with the whole of Lawrence; and includes part of J.C.F. Littlewood's 'Son and Lover', first published in the *Cambridge Quarterly* in 1969–70. This is the most challenging modern essay.

Among recent books, Michael Black: *D.H. Lawrence: the Early Fiction* (1986) places *Sons and Lovers* in the context of the other early novels and short stories, and gives particular emphasis to continuities and developments in the uses of imagery. Michael Black: *D. H. Lawrence: The Early Philosophical Works* (1992) analyses the 'Foreword' as the opening statement of a many times rewritten philosophy. Michael Bell: *D. H. Lawrence: Language and Being* (Cambridge, 1992) is a general study of Lawrence from a point of view influenced by German phenomenology and recent thought about anthropology, myth and language. Parts of this present study are indebted to discussion with Dr Bell.

Special thanks to Dr Lindeth Vasey for suggesting many improvements to this book. I am much indebted to her scholarship and care.

Printed in the United Kingdom
by Lightning Source UK Ltd.
105278UKS00001B/12